STEEL SPINE, CALM HEART

STEEL SPINE, CALM HEART

The Foundations of Masculine Frame

DARRIN ELFORD

Steel Spine, Calm Heart: The Foundations of Masculine Frame

ISBN: 978-1-991363-53-4 (Paperback)

eISBN: 978-1-991363-54-1 (E-Book)

First edition

Acknowledgements

No man becomes who he is alone. And this book—like the principles it contains—is the product of not just my own journey, but of the men and mentors, the challenges and breakdowns, the quiet moments and sharp awakenings that shaped me along the way.

To the **men who walk the talk**—the grounded, the stoic, the calm leaders who lead not through volume, but through vision—I thank you. Your presence, even in passing, taught me what real masculine strength looks like. You reminded me that leadership is earned, not given, and that power is best carried with humility.

To my **brothers and peers**, who challenged me, called me out, and called me up—you sharpened my edges. You reminded me that iron sharpens iron, and without tension, there is no transformation.

To the **women in my life**, whose intuition and depth offered balance to my intensity—thank you for showing me the necessity of harmony between strength and warmth, presence and compassion.

To my **readers**, especially the men ready to step into a new standard—thank you. Your hunger for growth, for depth, for something real, is the reason this book exists. You are the reason I kept writing when it would have been easier to stay silent. My hope is that these pages meet you where you are and walk with you into who you're becoming.

To the **great thinkers, warriors, and philosophers**—from Marcus Aurelius to Miyamoto Musashi, from Viktor Frankl to modern-day teachers of masculinity—you lit the way when the world felt fogged with noise. Your clarity and courage helped me find mine.

And finally, to the younger version of myself—the one who didn't yet know his power, who second-guessed his voice, who felt the weight of trying to be everything but didn't yet know how to be himself—you were never broken. You were only waiting to remember who you are.

May this book be a guide, a mirror, and a challenge to every man ready to carry himself with strength, stillness, and soul. And may we all continue to walk the world differently.

With respect and resolve,

Darrin Elford

Table of Contents

Introduction: The Calm Force That Shapes the World

What is Masculine Frame?

Masculine frame is not about pretending. It's not a performance, a costume, or a collection of alpha-male clichés. It's the unshakable core of a man who knows who he is—and never hands that over to anyone else.

Masculine frame is the **energetic posture** of self-possession. It's the calm in chaos, the gravity in a world spinning too fast, the silent authority in a room full of noise. You don't shout it. You don't explain it. You simply live it—and the world responds accordingly.

A man with masculine frame doesn't chase approval. He **leads with presence**. He doesn't crumble when tested. He holds his ground—not to dominate, but because his internal world is already settled. His emotions are not suppressed; they're **disciplined**. His power doesn't come from overpowering others, but from mastering himself.

Masculine frame is how a man **regulates his energy** and **projects his identity**—in relationships, in business, in crisis, in solitude. It's how he maintains emotional and psychological sovereignty, no matter the external pressure.

If you want a simple definition:

Masculine frame is the invisible structure of strength, clarity, and emotional control that makes a man immovable in the face of chaos.

You've seen men who have it. They walk into a room and **something shifts**. Not because they're the loudest, tallest, or most attractive—but because they are aligned, grounded, and fully embodied. They are **anchored** while others drift. Calm while others flinch. Focused while others scatter.

And here's the truth: **You can cultivate this.** Frame isn't reserved for the genetically blessed or the naturally confident. It's a **discipline**—a blueprint you can learn, build, and refine every day. This book is that blueprint.

We are not here to create a louder version of you. We are here to **build a stronger, quieter, more powerful version** of you. A version rooted so deeply that no woman, no boss, no critic, no failure can take it away.

Masculine frame is not about looking strong. It's about **being unshakeable**. And that starts now.

The Myth of Machismo vs. he Reality of Grounded Power

There's a dangerous illusion being sold to men today—a loud, shallow caricature of masculinity dressed in overcompensation. It's the man who talks too much, flexes too hard, dominates to hide his insecurity, and confuses control with power. This is **machismo**—and it's a myth.

Machismo is performative. It's a mask worn by the insecure, a shell built around fear. It postures. It provokes. It demands respect because it hasn't earned it. At its core, machismo is fragile. It's reactive. It's what a man does when he doesn't know who he is, so he tries to be what he thinks he should be.

But **grounded power**—real masculine power—doesn't need to posture.

Grounded power **doesn't seek validation**. It doesn't bark orders or dominate every conversation. It doesn't swing from aggression to collapse the moment it's challenged. Grounded power is **still**, not stagnant. It's **quiet**, not passive. It's **intense**, but never chaotic.

The man rooted in grounded power understands that **true strength is restraint**. He knows that silence can be louder than shouting. That clarity is more compelling than charisma. That leadership isn't about being followed—it's about embodying a standard that others naturally rise to.

The difference between machismo and masculine frame is the difference between **noise and signal**.

Machismo tries to impress. Masculine frame **doesn't need to**. Machismo is for show. Masculine frame is **for life**.

This book isn't about teaching you how to look strong. It's about building the kind of man who **is strong**—emotionally, psychologically, energetically. We're not layering false confidence over fear. We're doing the deep internal work that creates **unshakable presence**.

You'll find that the loudest men often lack the most inner structure. And you'll come to see that the most grounded men can move nations with a whisper. Because grounded power doesn't announce itself. It arrives—and everything changes.

Why Frame is the Foundation of Influence and Respect

Influence isn't something you ask for. Respect isn't something you chase. **They are byproducts of the frame you hold.**

In every interaction, there's a silent negotiation of power happening. Who leads? Who follows? Who adjusts? Who stands firm? Whether it's a conversation with a woman, a boardroom decision, or a standoff with your own self-doubt— the man who holds **frame** determines the outcome.

What is frame, in this context? It's your psychological position. Your emotional stance. Your inner reality projected outward. **Frame is the invisible boundary that tells the world who you are—and how you are to be treated.**

A man with frame doesn't need to argue for his value. His **presence communicates certainty**. His calmness under pressure makes him the emotional anchor for others. He doesn't flinch in discomfort. He doesn't compromise on his values to avoid conflict. Because of this, he becomes a natural point of gravity—people orbit him, not the other way around.

Without frame, a man gets pulled into other people's chaos. He reacts instead of leads. He seeks approval instead of commanding respect. He's easily thrown off by opinions, rejection, or confrontation—because his center isn't strong. He may have talent. He may even have ambition. But without frame, **his influence leaks**.

Now here's the hard truth:

If you do not hold your own frame, someone else will hold it for you. And if you constantly bend to fit into someone else's world, you will never build one of your own.

The man who has mastered masculine frame becomes unshakable not because life gets easier—but because he no longer negotiates who he is. His influence rises because people trust his steadiness. His respect grows because he operates from truth. Not performance. Not fear. Not ego.

Frame is the **foundation of influence**, because people follow clarity, not confusion. It is the **foundation of respect**, because strength—when grounded in authenticity—cannot be ignored.

This book isn't about tricks, tactics, or how to manipulate others. It's about becoming the kind of man who doesn't need to. Because his **presence speaks louder than persuasion**.

How to Use This Book

This is not a book you read once and put on the shelf. This is a **manual for transformation**—meant to be studied, revisited, and integrated.

Each chapter is a building block. You may come into this book thinking you just want to improve your presence or become more charismatic. But by the time you finish, you'll understand that masculine frame is not about isolated traits—it's a **system**. A structure. A way of being.

You'll see how **voice, silence, authority, charisma,** and **gravitas** are all interconnected. You'll understand that **authenticity, stoicism,** and **groundedness** are not soft concepts—they're your internal armor. And you'll realize that true **power** and **influence** can only flow from a man who has learned to lead himself.

Here's how to get the most from this book:

1. **Read Actively, Not Passively**

   Don't just absorb the words—**challenge yourself**. Highlight insights. Journal your reactions. Pause and ask: *"Where do I see this in my life? Where do I lack it?"* This book is a mirror, not just a message.

2. **Do the Work**

   Each chapter will include **practical steps**, exercises, and mindset shifts. These are not optional. Masculine frame isn't built in your mind—it's forged in your behavior. If you want results, you must **practice the discipline**.

3. **Take It One Frame at a Time**

   Some chapters will feel familiar. Others will confront you. That's the point. This isn't about rushing to the end. It's about building **layer by layer**, like a craftsman laying stone. Mastery doesn't come through speed—it comes through depth.

4. **Revisit the Foundations**

   Frame is not something you "get" and then forget. It's a **daily posture**. You'll fall out of frame. You'll forget who you are. When that happens, return to this book. Reread. Reflect. Recalibrate. Growth is not linear—it's cyclical.

5. **Lead Yourself First**

   This book will help you influence others, lead more effectively, and command deeper respect—but that starts with **you**. The man who cannot govern himself has no business trying to lead anyone else.

You don't need to become someone else. You need to **strip away everything that's not you**—the conditioning, the fear, the noise—until only what's solid remains. That's your frame. That's your power. Let's build it.

1

The Power of Tone – Deep Voice

The Psychology of Vocal Authority

Before a word leaves your mouth, your voice has already made a statement. Tone isn't just about how you sound—it's about what people feel when you speak. It communicates confidence, credibility, and composure—or the complete absence of them.

In human psychology, your voice signals where you stand in the social hierarchy **instantly**. Long before people decide whether they like you, agree with you, or want to follow you, they're unconsciously asking:

"Do I trust him? Do I respect him? Do I feel safe—or led—in his presence?"

Your tone answers before you do. Think of your voice as **energetic posture**. A shallow, high, or rushed voice suggests nervousness, self-doubt, or submission. A deep, calm, and resonant tone, on the other hand, **signals control**. Not domination—but grounded composure. It tells people, "I am settled within myself. I'm not chasing approval. I own this space."

Psychologists call this **paralanguage**—the nonverbal layer of communication that includes tone, pitch, pace, and pauses. Studies have shown that when it comes to influence, **how** you say something often carries more weight than **what** you say.

A man with masculine frame understands this. He **speaks slower**, because he's not in a rush to prove himself. He **uses pauses**, because he knows silence builds tension and gravity. He **lowers his pitch**, not artificially, but from a place of breath and centeredness.

He doesn't speak to fill silence—he speaks to create impact.

Why This Matters:

In high-stakes situations—business, conflict, attraction—people make snap judgments. They're not just listening to your logic. They're feeling your energy. If your voice shakes, cracks, or speeds up under pressure, it signals internal instability. But a **steady voice calms the room**. It becomes the emotional anchor.

That's vocal authority. It isn't about being loud. It's about being **clear, calm, and commanding**—without trying too hard. When you speak from your core—not your throat, not your ego—you don't need to convince. Your voice **becomes the message**.

How Tone Shapes Perception

Words are surface. **Tone is the undercurrent.**

You can say the same sentence with two different tones and evoke two entirely different reactions. One builds trust. The other triggers doubt. One draws people in. The other makes them pull away. That's the invisible power of tone—it shapes how people **perceive you**, even before they consciously interpret your words.

Your tone sends a **signal** about your emotional state. And here's the catch: the world believes the signal more than the sentence.

Say, *"I'm good,"* with a calm, low, steady tone—and people believe you. Say the same words with a rushed, shaky tone—and they instinctively sense you're not okay. The words didn't change. The tone changed everything.

Tone Communicates Frame Before You Do

In masculine frame, your tone becomes an extension of your internal world. When you're grounded, your tone reflects clarity and presence. When you're needy or reactive, your tone betrays insecurity—even if your words sound confident on paper.

That's why men who try to sound "alpha" often fail. Their words may be assertive, but their tone leaks desperation, anger, or approval-seeking. And people feel that. It repels rather than commands.

In contrast, the man with true frame **doesn't rush, doesn't rise in pitch, doesn't overexplain.** He speaks slowly—not because he's unsure, but because he's in control. He pauses—not because he's blank, but because he understands **his presence creates gravity.**

Tone is the gateway to how others **emotionally experience** you. In leadership, a composed tone fosters trust. In attraction, it conveys mystery, calm dominance, and control. In conflict, it sets the emotional tone of the exchange—cool head or chaos.

Your Voice Is Always Telling a Story

Here's the truth: every time you speak, you are **telling the world how to treat you.** Your tone tells people if they can challenge you, trust you, rely on you, or walk all over you. It signals if you're centered—or easily thrown off.

You can't fake this with clever phrases. But you **can train** it. When your tone matches your inner strength, people stop questioning you. They start feeling you. And once people **feel your certainty**, they stop resisting your presence. They start aligning with it.

Exercises to Deepen and Strengthen Your Voice

A deep, powerful voice isn't about genetics. It's about **breath, awareness, and consistency**. You don't need to be born with a Barry White bass to command respect—you need to learn how to speak from your **core**, not your throat.

Most men speak from the upper chest or even their head—resulting in a thin, nasal, or tense tone. A masculine voice resonates from **low in the body**—from the diaphragm, not the vocal cords alone. The difference is subtle to the ear, but **massive in impact**.

21

Below are proven exercises to help you deepen, steady, and strengthen your voice over time:

◆ 1. Diaphragmatic Breathing (The Foundation of Vocal Power)

What it does: Activates the diaphragm, deepens your breath, and supports vocal strength.

How to do it:

- Lie on your back or sit upright in a chair.

- Place one hand on your chest and one on your lower belly.

- Inhale through your nose, drawing air **into your belly**, not your chest.

- The belly should rise as you inhale, and fall as you exhale.

- Breathe slowly and deeply for 5–10 minutes daily.

Why it matters: Diaphragmatic breathing fuels your voice with depth and steadiness. It also calms your nervous system—essential for keeping frame under pressure.

◆ 2. The "Hum and Drop" Warm-Up

What it does: Helps you find your natural vocal depth and relax tension in the throat.

How to do it:

- Take a deep breath into your diaphragm.

- Gently hum on the exhale (like "mmm"), and allow the hum to vibrate through your chest.

- After humming for a few seconds, **drop into a simple phrase** like: *"I am here."*

- *"This is my voice."*

- Feel the vibration in your chest when you speak.

Why it matters: This trains you to speak from your chest, not your head. Over time, this unlocks more resonance and gravitas in your tone.

3. Slow Speak Training

What it does: Develops control, presence, and vocal authority.

How to do it:

- Choose a short paragraph or phrase you know well (e.g. a quote or your personal mission statement).

- Read or speak it **at 50% your normal speaking speed.**

- Focus on **pausing naturally** between phrases.

- Keep your tone steady, relaxed, and deliberate.

Why it matters: Speed is often a symptom of nervousness. Slow speech conveys confidence, intention, and frame.

4. Daily Low-Tone Practice

What it does: Builds vocal muscle memory for deeper tone.

How to do it:

- In the morning or before key interactions, speak 5–10 powerful phrases out loud in a **low, controlled tone**. Examples:

  - *"I speak with presence."*

  - *"My voice is grounded and clear."*

  - *"I lead with calm."*

- Focus on resonance—not volume.

Bonus: Record and listen back occasionally. You'll start hearing your progression over time.

◆ 5. Posture and Chest Expansion

What it does: Improves airflow and resonance.

How to do it:

- Stand tall with your shoulders slightly back and spine neutral.

- Take a few deep breaths with your chest open.

- Practice speaking with your body relaxed but **upright and alert**.

Why it matters: A compressed posture restricts your breath and tone. Confidence is heard—but also seen.

Don't try to force a deep voice overnight. That sounds fake. **Train it. Practice it. Live in it.** Your authentic tone will deepen naturally as you become more grounded in your breath, body, and presence. And when your voice comes from that place—**people listen differently.**

Breathing, Posture and Projection

A powerful voice doesn't start in the throat. It starts in the **body**. To speak with authority, you must first build the **physical foundation** that supports it. Without proper breathing and posture, your voice will always be limited—weak, tense, rushed, or uneven. But when your breath is deep, your body aligned, and your projection purposeful, your voice becomes a **force**.

This section ties it all together: breath, posture, and projection—three essential elements of vocal dominance.

1. Breathing: Speak from the Ground, Not the Throat

Breath is your **fuel**. When your breathing is shallow (chest breathing), your voice becomes strained or high-pitched under stress. But when you engage **diaphragmatic breathing**, your voice gains power without tension.

Practice this rhythm:

- Inhale through your nose for 4 seconds

- Hold for 2 seconds

- Exhale slowly for 6 seconds

Then speak a phrase while maintaining calm, full breath support.

Result: More vocal endurance, resonance, and emotional control—because when your breath is steady, your **frame is steady**.

2. Posture: Align Your Frame with Your Voice

Posture isn't just about looking confident—it's about creating space for your voice to flow.

Stand or sit like this:

- Feet shoulder-width apart

- Spine neutral, not slouched or overly stiff

- Shoulders slightly back, chest open

- Head upright and relaxed

This posture keeps your lungs and diaphragm unrestricted and signals **inner stability** to everyone around you.

Bonus: People subconsciously mirror posture. When yours radiates composure, others feel it—and respond to it.

◆ 3. Projection: Fill the Space Without Forcing

Projection is not volume. It's **energy directed with intention**.

Men who lack frame either mumble (under-projected) or yell (overcompensated). Neither commands respectTrue projection feels **effortless**—like your voice is carried on a wave of calm energy that fills the space naturally.

Try this:

Imagine your voice reaching the back wall of a room—not by shouting, but by sending it there with breath and clarity. Focus on speaking *through* the room, not just into the air in front of you.

Pro tip: Use your eyes when projecting. Speak *to someone specific*, not to everyone in general. This increases connection and focus.

◆ The Body Is the Voice

Your breath supports your tone. Your posture grounds your presence. Your projection expresses your **internal certainty**.

These aren't just physical techniques. They are **embodied traits of masculine frame**. When you align your voice with your body and breath, you move from sounding confident to **being confident**.

You don't just take up space. You **own it**.

2

The Strength of Silence

Why Stillness Commands Attention

In a world addicted to noise, **stillness is power**. Every day, we're bombarded with people fighting to be seen, heard, liked, followed. They talk fast, move nervously, over-explain, overshare, and overcompensate—hoping that if they just do *enough*, they'll be noticed. But the man who is **still**, who is silent, who moves with purpose instead of urgency—**he stands out** without even trying.

Why? Because stillness is a signal. It says: *I am not chasing. I am not threatened. I am not seeking validation. I'm already grounded.* That kind of energy is rare—and people feel it immediately.

Stillness isn't passive. It's not doing nothing. It's **choosing not to react**. It's choosing not to fill every space with words or motion. And in that space, something powerful happens: **others lean in**. They become more attentive. They start to feel your presence—not because you're trying to be seen, but because you're entirely **centered**.

In masculine frame, stillness is a form of leadership. When everyone else is flinching, fidgeting, or over-talking, the man who remains calm and composed becomes the **emotional anchor**. He doesn't need to impose himself. His restraint *is* the dominance.

Think about it:

- In a tense meeting, who commands the room? The man speaking rapidly... or the one who speaks rarely but with weight?

- In a social setting, who holds court? The one telling jokes non-stop... or the one who's composed, observant, and speaks only when it matters?

- In an argument, who holds power? The one who yells… or the one who stays still and unbothered?

Stillness commands attention because it's rare. But more than that—it reveals mastery. **Mastery over emotion. Mastery over environment. Mastery over self.** It tells the world you don't need to hustle for respect—you **already have it.**

Mastering the Pause: Timing and Tension

The pause is one of the most powerful tools in masculine communication—yet almost no one uses it. Why? Because silence makes most people uncomfortable. They rush to fill it. They blurt, explain, ramble, or retreat. But the man with frame doesn't fear the pause. He **uses** it. The pause creates **tension**—and tension creates **focus**.

When you speak without pausing, you flood the space with noise. People tune out. But when you pause—intentionally, confidently—you create a moment of **impact**. People lean in. Their nervous system pays attention. They feel the shift in energy. That's the psychology of the pause: it signals that what's coming next is **worth hearing**.

- **What the Pause Says Without Words**

When you pause before responding, it tells others:

- You are not reactive.

- You're comfortable with silence.

- You're thinking, not just reacting.

- You don't feel pressure to rush or perform.

When you pause after a statement, it tells others:

- What you said matters.

- You're letting it land.

- You own the room, not just your words.

The pause is power because it disrupts the rhythm people expect. It slows things down. And in that space, **your presence expands**.

◆ Timing Is Leadership

Leaders don't rush. Men with frame don't scramble. They **control time** by controlling their pacing.

Here's how you apply this:

- **Before you speak,** pause for one beat longer than feels natural. Let the room settle around you.

- **Mid-sentence,** use short pauses to create weight: *"There's a difference... between leading... and performing."*

- **After delivering a key point,** stop. Let silence do the rest.

You'll feel the tension build. That's good. That's where your authority lives.

◆ Pauses in Conflict and Intensity

In high-stakes moments—disagreements, emotional tension, confrontation—the pause becomes even more powerful. When others escalate, the man who pauses before he speaks demonstrates **absolute control**.

He doesn't react. He doesn't panic. He makes others wait—and in doing so, **shifts the power dynamic** without raising his voice or making a scene.

Final Note:

The pause is not empty. It's **full**—of control, clarity, and presence. It's not weakness. It's a demonstration of your **emotional authority**. Every time you speak, you have a choice: Rush to fill the space... or **own the silence before and after your words**. When you master the pause, your words no longer chase attention. They **command** it.

How to Speak Less but Mean More

In the age of endless chatter, the ability to speak less and **mean more** is a defining trait of men who command respect. While most people fill every silence with noise, the man with masculine frame understands that **brevity is a form of strength**.

Why does speaking less hold so much power? Because it's **intentional**. Because it shows **confidence**. Because it demonstrates **mastery over the urge to fill space** with inconsequential words.

The real art of speaking is knowing when to say something—and more importantly, when **not** to. By **paring down your words**, you elevate your impact. You show that your words have weight, that they're carefully chosen, and that you're not desperate to be heard.

◆ The Power of Precision

Speaking less doesn't mean becoming a mute—it means becoming **deliberate**. When you speak with precision, every word is a statement. Every sentence has meaning. You no longer waste energy on unnecessary explanations or overcompensating. Your words land with **certainty**, not guesswork.

How to do this:

- **Think before you speak.** Resist the impulse to respond immediately. Take a moment to compose your thoughts.

- **Strip away fluff.** Eliminate filler words like "um," "like," or "you know." Each unnecessary word dilutes your message.

- **Choose your words wisely.** Instead of explaining yourself, make clear statements. "This is how we move forward" instead of "I think we should maybe try this..."

◆ Less Is More in Conflict

In heated discussions or conflict, the less you speak, the more your message carries.

Why?

Because when you speak too much in conflict, you dilute your message and your authority. You risk appearing defensive or unsure. But when you speak concisely and **calmly**, you demonstrate control. You don't need to fill every silence with words; your **composure** and your **brevity** do the talking for you.

How to do this:

- **Pause before responding.** The silence gives you time to collect your thoughts, and it forces others to listen more intently when you speak.

- **Make a strong statement.** Instead of debating every point, choose one or two key phrases that assert your position clearly. Say less—but say it with **conviction**.

◆ The Influence of Silence Between Words

When you speak less, your words have **more room to breathe**. They're not lost in a sea of chatter—they stand out. Silence amplifies your message, creating anticipation for your next words. This is the difference between a man who speaks constantly to be heard, and one who speaks sparingly, but with authority.

How to use this principle:

- **Pause for effect** between your key points. Give the room time to process.

- When you've made your point, don't feel compelled to explain it further. Let the **impact** of your words settle.

- **Avoid over-explaining.** If someone asks for more details, answer with precision. You don't need to prove your intelligence—let your words stand on their own merit.

◆ **Silence as a Powerful Statement**

There's a profound **strength in silence** that many overlook. Sometimes, saying nothing at all communicates more than a thousand words. It shows that you don't feel the need to convince others of your worth. It shows you're **secure in your own presence**.

In a group, when everyone is over-explaining, the man who **chooses silence** doesn't feel left out—he **chooses the space**. He controls the room not by filling it with his voice, but by **commanding presence without uttering a word**.

Final Note:

Speaking less is not about being evasive or passive. It's about **intentionally choosing when to engage**. Every word you speak has a cost—don't waste it. The more you practice speaking less, the more your words will **mean**. And when your words mean more, your **presence** becomes the force people respond to.

Listening as a Dominant Trait

In a world that celebrates talking, the man who listens is often the one who leads. Most people talk to be heard. But the truly dominant, grounded man **listens to understand**—not just to respond. His listening isn't passive; it's active, engaging, and intentional. When he listens, he gathers information, reads between the lines, and most importantly, **takes control of the conversation without uttering a word**.

Why? Because listening is not just a skill—it's a form of power. When you listen with full attention, you are sending a message to the speaker:

You matter. Your words are worth my time. I am fully present with you.

This builds **trust** and **connection**. It makes others feel heard, understood, and valued. And without ever speaking, you've become the focal point of the exchange.

◆ The Power of Focused Listening

When you listen intently, you gain the power to influence without exerting any force. While others rush to speak, you take a step back, allowing the conversation to unfold at its own pace. This not only allows you to **gather more information** than those around you, but it also lets you **control the tempo** of the interaction.

How to do this:

- **Give your full attention** to the speaker. Let go of distractions—your phone, your thoughts, your inner monologue.

- **Stay present in the moment.** Don't rush to formulate your response while someone is still talking. Let them finish fully before you speak.

- **Use minimal verbal cues.** Nod occasionally, make eye contact, and give small affirmations like "I see" or "Interesting." But don't interrupt or fill the space with unnecessary words.

By doing this, you not only show respect to the speaker but also place yourself in a position of control. You **guide** the conversation through your attentiveness.

◆ Listening as an Indicator of Confidence

The more secure you are in yourself, the more you can listen without needing to **prove** your worth through constant talking. A man who listens deeply doesn't feel the need to fill every silence with his voice. His confidence is **silent**, rooted in the **certainty** that what he chooses to say will carry far more weight than a string of empty words.

How to do this:

- **Resist the urge to speak first.** Instead of jumping in, wait for a moment of silence or a natural opening.

- **Pause before responding.** Give the conversation room to breathe. When you do speak, your words will seem more thoughtful, impactful, and intentional.

People can sense **insecurity** in those who can't stop talking. They're uncomfortable with silence. But the man who can listen without feeling the need to dominate the dialogue **commands respect**.

◆ Listening to Read People

The art of listening is not just about hearing words—it's about understanding the **intent** behind them. When you listen closely, you gather clues about a person's emotions, their priorities, and their vulnerabilities. This is invaluable information in any situation, whether in business negotiations, personal relationships, or social interactions.

How to do this:

- **Listen for the underlying emotion.** People often say more than they intend in the spaces between their words. Pay attention to what's unsaid.

- **Watch body language.** The way someone moves or holds themselves can tell you far more than what comes out of their mouth.

- **Ask the right questions.** Probing questions show that you're truly engaged and seeking to understand the full context of a conversation.

When you can listen not only to **what** is said but **how** it's said, you position yourself as a **master communicator**, able to influence situations and people with ease.

◆ Listening to Strengthen Relationships

Strong relationships are built on trust, and trust is built on **mutual understanding**. When you listen actively, you allow others to feel **seen** and **valued**—and that builds a strong foundation for collaboration, respect, and influence.

People will be drawn to you because they feel heard, and when people feel heard, they are more likely to follow your lead.

How to do this:

- **Make others feel important.** Use phrases like, "Tell me more about that," or "I'd love to hear your thoughts."

- **Validate their experience.** Even if you disagree, acknowledge the other person's perspective. A simple "I see where you're coming from" can go a long way in building rapport.

- **Be patient and give space.** Don't rush the conversation. Allow others to speak freely, and show that you value their input.

Through active listening, you create a sense of **psychological safety**—a space where people feel comfortable sharing and engaging, knowing their voice matters.

Final Note:

The dominant man doesn't need to raise his voice to be heard. He doesn't need to dominate the conversation. He doesn't need to be the loudest or the quickest to speak.

Instead, he listens. He listens with intention. And in doing so, he builds connection, influence, and trust.

By choosing when to speak and when to listen, you control the flow of energy in any conversation. The more you practice this art, the more others will be drawn to your centered, grounded presence.

Avoiding Nervous Talk and Over-Explaining

Nothing kills masculine presence faster than nervous talk. It's one of the most common ways men leak frame—often without realizing it. They speak too fast, say too much, and offer excessive detail in an effort to sound smart, be liked, or avoid conflict. But instead of creating clarity, they create confusion. Instead of appearing confident, they appear insecure.

At its core, nervous talk is self-soothing. It's the verbal equivalent of fidgeting. It doesn't serve the listener—it serves your own discomfort. And people can feel it. Every extra word you add out of fear weakens the impact of the ones that matter.

◆ Nervous Talk Signals a Lack of Frame

When you can't sit with silence… when you over-explain basic decisions… when you keep talking because you're afraid someone might misunderstand you—you're signaling that you don't trust yourself.

And if you don't trust yourself, why should anyone else? Whether it's in leadership, dating, negotiation, or everyday interaction, men who talk nervously give away power. They reveal that they're not grounded, that they need external validation, and that they're uncomfortable with tension.

A man with a steel spine doesn't need to *prove* he's right. He doesn't need to *beg* for agreement. He speaks clearly, says what needs to be said—and then lets the silence do the rest.

◆ The Over-Explanation Trap

Over-explaining is one of the most subtle but damaging habits for men trying to develop authority.

You make a decision… then explain why. Then justify it. Then explain again— just to make sure no one's offended or confused. But what you're really doing is seeking permission. You're trying to control how others perceive you, instead of trusting your own judgment.

Over-explaining weakens leadership. It invites unnecessary debate. It undermines your own clarity. In truth, strong statements don't need backup dancers.

Compare:

- ✗ "Well, I was just thinking that maybe if we tried this, it could work… I mean, unless anyone thinks otherwise."

- ☑ "This is the direction we're taking."

One shows hesitation. The other shows decisiveness.

◆ How to Break the Habit

Breaking nervous talk and over-explaining is about self-awareness and deliberate restraint. Here's how to train it:

1. **Speak... then stop.**

   When you've made your point, resist the urge to add more. Say it. Shut up. Let your words settle.

2. **Use the Rule of One.**

   State your point once, clearly and directly. If someone asks for more, elaborate *then*—not preemptively.

3. **Breathe before you respond.**

   Nervous talk is often a symptom of anxious energy. A 2-second pause gives you control. It slows your tempo and centers your delivery.

4. **Let silence do the work.**

   After speaking, don't race to fill the quiet. Hold your ground. Let others respond. This shows confidence in what you said—and in yourself.

5. **Trust your words.**

   You don't need to *convince* when you speak from clarity. You don't need to repeat when your presence is strong.

◆ Confidence Is Concise

A man with masculine frame understands: the fewer words he uses, the more each one matters.

He doesn't repeat himself. He doesn't dilute his point. He doesn't explain his value—he embodies it. Remember: you're not here to be understood by everyone. You're here to stand in your truth, speak with calm precision, and let others adjust to your gravity.

Final Note:

Cutting out nervous talk is not about saying less—it's about saying what matters and standing by it. When you eliminate over-explaining, you create space. And in that space, people begin to take you more seriously—because they feel the weight of your words.

The man who speaks with intention doesn't chase approval. He already has respect.

3

Magnetic Masculinity – Charisma & Charm

The Science of Attraction: Subtle Signals

Charisma isn't loud. It doesn't announce itself with a bullhorn. The most magnetic men aren't the ones talking the most—they're the ones **radiating something deeper**.

True attraction isn't built on tricks, lines, or forced charm. It's built on **subtle, subconscious signals** that speak directly to the human nervous system. These cues tell others:

This man is confident. This man is grounded. This man is safe… but also a challenge. And they don't need to be said. They're **felt**. Let's break down what those signals are—and how to embody them in a way that's authentic and powerful.

◆ **1. Calmness Under Pressure**

The nervous system responds to emotional energy. When you're anxious, fidgety, or reactive, others feel that instability—even if you're saying all the right things.

But when you remain **calm in uncertainty**, you emit a frequency people crave. You signal that you're anchored, composed, and emotionally regulated. That creates a sense of **trust and mystery**. It's why women are drawn to unshakable men. It's not just strength—they're sensing **safety and polarity**.

Practice it:

- Slow your breathing in tense or high-energy settings.

- Hold eye contact with softness, not force.

- Let your movements be **minimal, relaxed, deliberate**.

◆ 2. Microexpressions and Body Language

Your face, posture, and gestures tell a story before your voice ever speaks. Small, unconscious behaviors either **pull people in** or signal discomfort.

Key charismatic signals:

- **Eyes relaxed** but alert. Not darting. Not blank.

- **Slight smirk** or micro-smile. Not fake enthusiasm—just a quiet "I know something" energy.

- **Open body posture**—shoulders back, chest relaxed, arms uncrossed.

- **Subtle mirroring** of the other person's energy, pace, or tone—done intuitively, not robotically.

Avoid: excessive blinking, touching your face, over-nodding, and filler movements that reveal tension or insecurity.

◆ 3. Vocal Tone and Tempo

As explored earlier, a deep, calm voice signals authority. But it also signals **attraction**, because it resonates with **low-frequency vibration**—which the human body interprets as dominance, certainty, and strength.

But even more important is **vocal tempo**. Charismatic men speak slowly, with intention. They pause. They don't rush to fill silence. This draws others in, because it signals that you're **comfortable with space**, and you're used to being listened to.

Practice it:

- Lower your voice at the end of your sentences (downward inflection).

- Pause before and after making a key point.

- Don't be afraid of silence—it creates tension and focus.

◆ 4. Presence: The Most Magnetic Force of All

True charisma is the result of one thing: **presence**. When you are fully here—fully in your body, fully in the moment—people feel it. Most are scattered, distracted, halfway between their thoughts and their phone. But the man who is **present** becomes rare. And what is rare becomes **valuable**.

When you're present:

- Your eyes connect, instead of scanning.

- Your responses are attuned, not rehearsed.

- Your body relaxes, and your energy settles.

Presence can't be faked. But it can be cultivated—through breath, stillness, and intention.

◆ Attraction Is Not Performed. It's Transmitted.

The most attractive men don't *try* to be attractive. They don't chase attention. They don't dominate conversations. They simply **show up as whole, grounded, complete**—and others feel pulled into their orbit.

That's the science of subtle signals:

- It's not what you say.

- It's what your energy is *saying for you*.

Final Thought:

You don't need to manufacture charm. You don't need to manipulate people into liking you. Magnetism begins when you stop trying to impress—and start **embodying who you are** with unapologetic calm.

People are drawn not to perfection, but to **presence**. Not to noise, but to **depth**. And not to performance—but to **realness**.

Body Language That Draws People In

Charisma doesn't start with words. It begins the moment you **enter a space**.

Long before you speak, your body is already communicating. It's telling people whether you're confident or uncertain, grounded or scattered, open or closed. And most of this communication happens beneath conscious awareness. It's **felt**, not processed.

That's why mastering charismatic body language isn't about being flashy or exaggerated. It's about learning to let your body say what your words **shouldn't have to**:

"I'm calm. I'm present. I belong here."

Let's break down the key elements of body language that naturally draw people in—without trying too hard, without performing, and without betraying your masculine frame.

◆ **1. Open Posture = Open Energy**

Your posture is your first introduction. Before anyone hears your name or your voice, they read your **stance**.

Commanding posture:

- Stand or sit with a straight spine, shoulders relaxed but slightly back.

- Keep your chest open—not puffed, not collapsed.

- Feet shoulder-width apart when standing, balanced and rooted.

Avoid:

- Hunched shoulders (signals insecurity).

- Crossed arms (signals defensiveness).

- Fidgeting or shifting weight constantly (signals nervous energy).

An open posture shows you're **receptive but grounded**—the perfect blend of strength and approachability.

2. The Magnetic Use of Eye Contact

Eye contact is one of the most **intimate and powerful tools** in masculine communication. It's not about staring someone down—it's about being **fully present** when your eyes meet.

How to use it:

- Hold soft, steady eye contact when listening and speaking.

- Break eye contact occasionally to avoid turning it into a challenge—but don't dart your eyes around nervously.

- Smile with your eyes, not just your mouth. This creates warmth and connection.

Bonus: When speaking to a group, land your gaze on one person at a time. This makes everyone feel seen, while anchoring your energy.

3. Relaxed, Controlled Movements

Fast, jerky, or excessive movement signals nervous energy. Magnetic men **move slowly and deliberately**, as if they are never in a rush. Each gesture has purpose.

Embody this by:

- Minimizing unnecessary hand gestures.

- Keeping your arms loose at your sides or gently resting when seated.

- Turning your full body toward the person you're engaging with—it shows you're not distracted.

Remember: Movement should match message. The calmer your energy, the more trust and curiosity you'll inspire.

◆ 4. The Power of Space: Don't Shrink Yourself

Magnetic body language is also about **owning your space**. Men who lack frame tend to shrink themselves—crossing their legs tightly, hunching forward, keeping their hands hidden. It's unconscious self-protection.

Instead:

- Take up your rightful space. Let your body breathe.

- When you sit, let your arms rest comfortably, feet grounded, shoulders broad.

- Don't apologize with your posture. You are **allowed to exist fully** in the room.

This doesn't mean spreading out aggressively. It means moving and holding yourself like a man who **doesn't ask for permission to be here**.

◆ 5. Controlled Facial Expression

Your face tells the truth even when your mouth lies. People read micro-expressions instinctively. Tension in the brow, clenched jaws, or forced smiles signal unease or inauthenticity.

Train a **resting face of calm confidence**:

- Neutral mouth, with a slight natural downturn or soft smirk.

- Unfurrowed brow.

- Eyes relaxed but alert.

You don't need to "perform" friendliness. Just remove tension, and let your natural presence rise.

You don't need to be the most attractive, tallest, or flashiest man in the room. You need to be the most **settled**, the most **embodied**, the most **present**. That's what body language communicates—without saying a word.

When your posture is strong, your movements are calm, and your eyes are focused, you send a subtle but unmistakable message: *"I'm not here to impress. I'm here to lead."* And that's the kind of presence people are naturally drawn to.

Humor, Warmth and Confidence Balance

Charisma isn't just about strength. It's about **balance**—the dance between edge and ease, gravity and levity, presence and play.

The most magnetic men have mastered a unique emotional cocktail: they are **confident**, but not arrogant. **Warm**, but not needy. **Funny**, but not performative.

They embody a rare mix that makes others feel both **challenged and safe**, respected and intrigued. Let's break down the three key ingredients—**humor, warmth**, and **confidence**—and how to calibrate them with masculine precision.

◆ Humor: The Doorway to Connection

Humor is social magic. When used well, it lowers defenses, bridges gaps, and makes people feel at ease in your presence. It signals intelligence, emotional agility, and most importantly—**non-neediness**.

The right kind of humor says:

"I don't need to take myself too seriously—because I'm secure in who I am."

But here's the key:

Charismatic men use humor **sparingly and strategically**. They're not court jesters. They don't chase laughs. Instead, they inject humor in moments of tension or to signal playfulness beneath their composed surface.

Guidelines for charismatic humor:

- Use **dry wit or observational humor**, not self-deprecation.

- Avoid trying too hard or making people laugh just to fill space.

- Be playful, not performative. Let your humor arise **organically**—never at the cost of your dignity or someone else's.

When used right, humor enhances your presence. When overused, it **diminishes your gravity**.

◆ **Warmth: The Strength of Approachability**

Some men think being masculine means being cold or stoic to the point of detachment. But true magnetic presence has **heat**. It's not icy—it's **grounded and warm**.

Warmth doesn't mean weakness. It means you can make others feel **seen and safe**—without sacrificing your edge. It's the look that says, *"I respect you."* It's the way you remember someone's name, hold eye contact with kindness, or offer a subtle smile when the moment calls for it.

Warmth **amplifies your charisma** because it makes your strength human.

Ways to cultivate warmth:

- Be genuinely curious about others. Ask real questions. Listen.

- Offer small, unforced compliments or acknowledgments.

- Keep your facial expression relaxed and your tone calm, even when being direct.

Warmth is what draws people closer. Strength alone might get their attention—but warmth is what **earns their trust**.

◆ Confidence: The Unshakable Core

Confidence is the **engine** behind both your humor and your warmth. It's what allows you to be playful without fear, kind without defensiveness, and silent without needing to fill the space.

Real confidence isn't loud. It doesn't seek validation. It's calm, controlled, and self-contained.

When you're confident:

- You speak when you choose—not to impress, but to **express**.

- You don't try to win people over—you let them experience you.

- You don't need to be liked to feel whole—you're already complete.

True charisma starts here—with the unshakable knowing that you don't need to perform for connection. You're already enough. And that belief, embodied, becomes a gravitational pull.

◆ The Balance Is the Magnetism

Any one of these traits in isolation can become a caricature:

- Too much humor = clown.

- Too much warmth = nice guy.

- Too much confidence = arrogance.

But the man who weaves all three into his presence—**strategic humor, subtle warmth, unshakable confidence**—is the one people are drawn to without knowing why.

He's light without being lightweight. He's kind without being weak. He's strong without being hard.

And most of all—he makes others **feel good** in his presence, without sacrificing his own integrity.

You don't have to choose between being powerful and being approachable. You don't have to choose between being respected and being liked. You simply have to show up **fully aligned**—with humor to disarm, warmth to connect, and confidence to anchor it all.

That's the balance that creates **undeniable charisma**. That's **magnetic masculinity**.

Becoming Effortlessly Memorable

The most memorable men rarely try to be. They don't chase attention, overshare, or dominate the conversation. They leave a lasting impression not because they push—but because they **pull**.

They pull people in with their presence, their calm, their clarity. They speak when it counts. They listen with full attention. They walk away—and others are still thinking about them.

To become effortlessly memorable, you don't need to be the loudest, the most charming, or the most visible. You need to be the most **centered**, the most **real**, and the most **tuned-in**.

Here's how.

◆ 1. Lead with Presence, Not Performance

People remember how you made them **feel**—not how hard you tried to impress them.

If you're performing, pushing for approval, or talking too much, you might get attention—but it won't last. What sticks in the mind is someone who is **fully present**, even in silence.

Memorable presence looks like this:

- Holding eye contact just a beat longer than most.

- Speaking calmly, even when others are animated.

- Standing or sitting with posture that says, *"I'm exactly where I should be."*

Presence is power. It's the invisible current that pulls people back to you—long after you've left the room.

2. Say Less, Say It Well

Words are like currency—the more carelessly you spend them, the less value they hold.

Memorable men **don't overshare**. They don't dominate the conversation. They speak with **precision**. They let their words land. And when they're done, they stop talking.

That restraint builds **mystery**. It suggests there's more beneath the surface. It makes people want to know more.

Speak in headlines. Drop meaningful insights with clarity and brevity. You'll be surprised how much more people remember when you say **less**, but with weight.

3. Make People Feel Seen

One of the fastest ways to become unforgettable? Make **others** feel unforgettable.

When you give someone your full attention—no phone, no scanning the room, no half-listening—you stand out immediately. In a distracted world, focused attention is rare. And rare is **memorable**.

How to practice this:

- Use people's names.

- Ask sincere, open-ended questions.

- Mirror their language subtly to build connection.

- Listen so well that you can recall small details later.

When someone feels seen by you, they feel **valued**. And people never forget the ones who made them feel valuable.

4. Anchor Your Identity in Calm Confidence

What makes someone unforgettable isn't a gimmick or technique—it's **depth**.

Depth comes from knowing who you are. What you stand for. What you don't tolerate. What you don't need to prove.

You become effortlessly memorable when you walk through the world with **calm certainty**, not as a man looking for validation—but as a man **already full**.

You're not looking to be impressive. You simply are—because you've done the inner work.

Final Note: Legacy Over Performance

Being memorable isn't about leaving people in awe. It's about leaving them **better**. A little calmer. A little more curious. A little more aware.

When you move through the world with clarity, grace, and grounded strength, people remember you—not because you demanded attention, but because you carried a presence that couldn't be ignored.

Be someone whose silence speaks louder than others' noise. Be the man who doesn't try to be memorable......and becomes unforgettable because of it.

Avoiding Neediness While Remaining Open

True charisma walks a razor's edge. On one side: warmth, openness, connection. On the other: neediness, approval-seeking, self-abandonment.

The difference between the two? Frame.

When a man has internal frame, he can be deeply present, emotionally attuned, and even vulnerable—without ever chasing approval. But without that inner foundation, what looks like openness quickly turns into energetic grasping. The room can feel it. The conversation shifts. The polarity breaks.

To remain open without being needy, you must give from a place of wholeness, not hunger.

◆ What Neediness Actually Is

Neediness isn't about wanting something—everyone wants connection, recognition, love, respect. That's human. Neediness is when your sense of self depends on getting it.

It sounds like:

- "Do they like me?"

- "Did I say the right thing?"

- "Why haven't they responded yet?"

- "What can I do to impress them?"

This internal script hijacks your energy. You start behaving not from grounded intention—but from subtle fear: fear of rejection, abandonment, insignificance. And people feel that. Not always consciously, but instinctively. Neediness repels because it signals unmet need that others are now being asked to manage.

◆ The Power of Detachment

To stay open while avoiding neediness, you must practice non-attachment to outcomes. This doesn't mean you don't care—it means your identity isn't on the line. You can be fully engaged in a moment, a connection, a conversation... and still remain unmoved if it doesn't go your way.

That's powerful. That's rare. That's magnetic.

Practice it like this:

- Engage, but don't chase.

- Compliment, but don't qualify yourself.

- Ask questions, but don't need validation.

- Be vulnerable, but don't offload responsibility for your feelings.

This is openness from strength—not from lack.

◆ Boundaries Create Polarity

Needy energy floods boundaries. It over-explains. It overshares. It wants to be understood—now. It clings. But grounded masculine openness honors space. It invites connection without demanding it. It knows when to speak, and when to step back and observe.

To cultivate this:

- Be slow to reveal too much too soon.

- Leave space in conversation. Let others come toward you.

- Be willing to walk away if the vibe doesn't feel aligned.

When you value yourself first, you teach others to value you too.

◆ Vulnerability Without Collapse

Being open doesn't mean being exposed. It means being available, but still intact.

A grounded man can say:

"Here's what I feel. Here's what I value. Here's where I stand."

But he never says:

"Please like me for it."

Vulnerability becomes magnetic when it's shared from fullness, not to get filled.

Examples:

- "I admire how present you are" (genuine warmth—not bait).

- "I value honesty. I'd rather hear the truth than be strung along" (clear, confident boundary—not emotional plea).

- "I've had my share of mistakes, and I've learned from every one" (ownership—not a veiled cry for sympathy).

You don't lose power by being real. You lose power by attaching your self-worth to someone else's response to your truth.

◆ **Final Note: Stand Open. Stay Whole.**

The masculine heart isn't cold—it's calm. It doesn't need to be closed off to be protected. It just needs to be anchored. When you stop trying to earn love or attention, and instead show up as love, as presence, as power, people feel safe around you—and pulled toward you.

That's how you become magnetic:

Not by needing something from the world, But by bringing something to it.

4

The CEO Effect – Executive Presence

What People Instantly Notice About You

Long before you speak, your presence has spoken. In the first seven seconds—often less—people are already making unconscious judgments about who you are, how much power you carry, and whether you're someone to follow... or forget. This is the realm of **executive presence**—and it begins with what others *feel* before they even understand why.

We like to believe we're judged by the substance of our words. In truth, we're judged by the **signals we send** without saying a thing. Executive presence doesn't start with talking. It starts with how you **enter the room**, how you **hold yourself**, and how you make others **feel in your presence**.

Here's what people instantly notice about you—and what it silently communicates about your leadership, confidence, and masculine frame.

◆ 1. Your Posture and Bearing

Your body broadcasts your identity. A man who carries himself with straight posture, shoulders relaxed, chin level—not forced, not stiff—signals **readiness**, **competence**, and **composure**. He doesn't shrink himself to be liked. He doesn't puff himself up to be feared. He simply owns his space with natural authority.

What people feel:

"He knows who he is. He's not here to prove it."

Compare that to someone slouched, fidgeting, or visibly uncomfortable in their body. Even without a word, it tells the room: *"I don't belong here."* People believe that message—because it came from **you**.

◆ 2. Your Energy and Pace

Speed is the signature of insecurity. Presence is revealed in **slowness**. Whether it's your walking pace, your eye contact, your reaction time, or the way you set down your phone—people track your tempo. When you move with deliberate calm, it signals **internal control**. When you rush, stumble, or over-animate, it leaks anxiety.

What people feel:

"He's centered. He's not reacting to the room—he's setting the tone."

That's how you command attention without needing to demand it: you slow the room down simply by being in it.

◆ 3. Your Eyes and Expression

People look to your face for the emotional temperature of the room. A CEO doesn't flinch, frown, or wear uncertainty across his forehead. He doesn't smile excessively to seek comfort. He radiates **composed alertness**—eyes clear, gaze steady, face relaxed.

What people feel:

"This man is calm under pressure. He sees clearly. He's not looking to be led— he's already leading."

Eye contact, especially, is a power tool. Used well, it signals credibility, presence, and calm dominance. Avoidance, on the other hand, suggests inner chaos or submission.

◆ 4. The Way You Occupy Space

Executive presence doesn't apologize. It doesn't ask permission to exist. People instantly sense whether you're comfortable being seen, or whether you're shrinking your presence to avoid judgment. A man with frame **owns the moment**—not arrogantly, but with quiet certainty. He takes his seat with confidence. He walks into a room with posture, purpose, and presence. He's not trying to be invisible—and he's not performing for attention either.

What people feel:

"He's not trying to earn the room. He already knows he belongs in it."

◆ 5. The Emotional Field You Radiate

People don't just hear your words—they feel your **emotional tone**. Are you tense, irritated, nervous, overeager? Or are you calm, steady, grounded?

The most powerful leaders project an invisible but undeniable force: **composure under pressure**. They can walk into a room filled with uncertainty and **regulate the energy**, not be ruled by it. Their emotional state becomes a stabilizing field for others. That's what makes them unforgettable.

What people feel:

"I don't know what it is… but I trust this man."

Final Thought: People Feel Your Frame Before They Hear It

Before you open your mouth, the room has already received its message. You can't fake this. You can't rehearse it. You must **become it**—by aligning your body, energy, and emotional presence to reflect the **inner clarity and leadership** you've built.

Your voice will matter. Your words will matter. But they will only land if your presence tells the room:

"I don't need to be the center of attention. I am the center of gravity."

That's executive presence. That's the CEO effect. And it starts the moment you walk in.

Dress, Demeanor and Dominance

Presence isn't just an inner state—it's a **visual language**. Long before you speak, the way you show up visually either reinforces your authority or weakens it. In environments where leadership and perception matter—boardrooms, negotiations, social arenas—your **appearance**, **behavior**, and **energy** speak volumes about who leads and who follows.

This isn't about vanity. It's about **signal clarity**. The masculine frame doesn't just rely on internal confidence—it projects it with **precision** through how you dress, how you carry yourself, and how you dominate space with calm, quiet force.

◆ Dress: Your Visual Authority

What you wear tells people how seriously to take you. It communicates standards, self-respect, and intentionality. Sloppy, loud, or trend-chasing outfits suggest a man who is either seeking validation or doesn't know who he is.

Masculine style isn't about being flashy—it's about being **fluent in power language**.

Key principles of dominant dress:

- **Fit over fashion**: Clothes should trace your frame without exaggerating it. Tailored, clean, structured lines signal clarity and order.

- **Minimalism = strength**: The man who wears fewer accessories, neutral tones, and timeless pieces says, *"I don't need to decorate power. I embody it."*

- **Grooming = discipline**: Neat hair, trimmed beard, clean nails, intentional scent—these details show self-respect and readiness.

You don't need a $5,000 suit to look like a leader. You need a body and wardrobe that say: *"I care. I notice. I choose."*

◆ Demeanor: The Vibe You Broadcast

Your demeanor is your **emotional tone made visible**. It's the way you stand in silence. The way you acknowledge someone with a nod. The way you walk into a room and make people feel your calm **before you speak**.

Dominant demeanor doesn't mean being aggressive, aloof, or overly serious. It means you radiate a grounded, settled authority that others **feel safe around— but never in control of**.

Elements of dominant demeanor:

- **Stillness**: Don't fidget. Don't gesture excessively. Still men are read as composed men.

- **Pacing**: Speak and move with deliberateness. Haste is the signature of someone who doesn't feel in control.

- **Polite detachment**: You're friendly, but not overly eager. You engage, but don't chase. You smile when *you choose to*, not when you're trying to be liked.

This is what makes people take a second look—not because you're loud, but because you're **undeniably present**.

◆ Dominance: The Subtle Expression of Power

Let's define this clearly: **Dominance isn't about intimidation**. It's not about barking orders or inflating your chest. True masculine dominance is **non-verbal, non-reactive, and non-needy**.

It's the quiet, steady confidence of a man who doesn't flinch, doesn't overexplain, and doesn't fight for control—because he already holds it internally.

Ways dominance expresses through presence:

- **Claiming space** without apology. Whether seated or standing, your body should reflect a man at ease in his own domain.

- **Making decisions** quickly and calmly. Indecision shrinks authority. Even a small choice made decisively amplifies presence.

- **Speaking last, speaking less**. Dominant men are often the most silent in the room—but when they speak, everyone listens.

Your dominance isn't about dominating others. It's about being so grounded, so self-contained, that others naturally **orient themselves around your gravity**.

A man's executive presence is most felt when his **outer presentation mirrors his inner authority**.

- Dress clean and sharp—not to impress, but to reflect your self-respect.

- Move with economy—not to perform, but to signal composure.

- Hold space—not to control, but to lead without needing to announce it.

When dress, demeanor, and dominance align, you become the man who doesn't fight for the spotlight—You **are** the spotlight.

Managing First Impressions

You never get a second chance at a first impression—because in most cases, you don't need one.

The masculine frame, when fully developed, doesn't ask for multiple exposures to be recognized. It hits *immediately*. The moment you walk in, people decide how to categorize you: leader or follower, grounded or reactive, asset or liability.

That impression is formed in **seconds**—and it's not rational. It's **instinctual**, based on subtle cues: how you enter a space, how you carry your energy, and what emotion you leave behind.

Executive presence means knowing how to make that first moment **land** with clarity, command, and control.

◆ The Instant Signals You Send

The human brain is wired to size others up rapidly. Your clothes, posture, facial expression, eye contact, tone, and even how you **pause** are all cues people use to assess you.

Within the first few seconds, they've decided:

- Whether you're confident or compensating.

- Whether you're high-status or trying to appear high-status.

- Whether you're grounded or grasping.

Masculine truth:

People aren't evaluating your *value*—they're evaluating your **certainty** about your value. That's what wins trust, respect, and space.

◆ Entering the Room with Authority

Before you say a word, you've already made your first impression.

Walk in with:

- **Slow, intentional pace** – Speed signals nervous energy. Calm, deliberate movement signals control.

- **Head up, eyes scanning confidently** – Not looking for approval, but observing the environment like a man who belongs.

- **Posture that breathes strength** – Chest relaxed but open, shoulders back, spine straight, no tension.

When you enter a room like you already own your space, people feel it. You don't have to "break the ice." You *are* the change in temperature.

◆ The Power of the First Words

Your first few words carry weight far beyond their content. Tone, tempo, and **calm confidence** are everything.

Tips for verbal first impressions:

- Speak slowly and clearly. Don't rush.

- Avoid filler words like "um," "like," or "you know." They dilute impact.

- Pause intentionally before and after your opening sentence. Silence amplifies authority.

- Smile with your eyes, not your mouth. Show warmth without submission.

When your voice lands with certainty and your face reads as unbothered, you've already won more influence than a dozen credentials could earn.

◆ High-Status Energy: Not Eager, Not Arrogant

The sweet spot for a commanding first impression is **non-neediness**. You're not trying to be liked, but you're not closed off either.

You're **receptive** without chasing. **Open** without oversharing. **Warm** without submissive laughter or fake smiles. **Present** without over-explaining. People remember men who embody that paradox: *welcoming, yet clearly whole without you.*

◆ Final Note: Build the Frame Before the Moment

You don't rise to the occasion—you fall to your level of preparation.

A powerful first impression doesn't start when you enter the room. It starts with the **daily discipline** of posture, stillness, tone, awareness, and self-respect. Build your internal world so consistently that when the moment comes, your **external signal is undeniable**.

First impressions are either accidental or engineered. A man of frame chooses the impression he makes—because he's already chosen who he is.

Walking into a Room with Presence

Most men enter a room the way they live their life—**unconsciously**, hoping not to be noticed too much, or overcompensating to be noticed too fast. But presence is not about being loud. It's not about being the center of attention. True masculine presence is about being **felt**, even before you're seen.

When you walk into a room with presence, you don't need to announce yourself. People's bodies turn, their eyes pause, their conversation slows—for reasons they can't articulate. That's not charisma. That's not image. That's **embodied power**.

This kind of presence can't be faked—but it can be trained. Here's how.

◆ 1. Own the Room Before You Enter It

Presence doesn't start at the doorway—it starts with **intention**. You must decide **who you are**, and how you will hold yourself, *before* you take your first step inside.

Ask yourself:

- "What energy am I bringing in?"

- "What outcome do I intend to shape?"

- "What kind of man do I choose to be in this space?"

This pre-frame aligns your body, breath, and behavior. Without it, you walk in reacting. With it, you walk in **leading**.

◆ 2. Slow Your Walk, Straighten Your Spine

Rushed movement signals anxiety. Confident movement is deliberate. When you walk into a room:

- Keep your spine upright and neutral—not stiff, not slouched.

- Drop your shoulders and let your chest open naturally.

- Walk at a steady, unhurried pace.

- Let your arms swing loosely but controlled at your sides.

You're not sneaking in, and you're not performing. You're **entering as if you already belong**—because you do.

◆ 3. Scan the Room, Don't Seek Approval

As you walk in, your eyes should calmly scan the room. Not darting, not searching—**observing**.

You're taking inventory of the environment with detached awareness. You're not looking to be seen; you're reading the energy, locating key players, and anchoring yourself in the moment.

What this communicates:

"I'm alert, but unbothered. I see everything, and I'm not trying to be anything."

Avoid rapid eye contact with everyone. Lock eyes with one or two people naturally and move on. Too much searching looks insecure. Too little looks avoidant. Presence is in the **middle path**.

◆ 4. Don't Fidget, Don't Rush to Speak

Once you've entered, resist the urge to do something. You don't need to prove you're confident—you need to **hold your center**.

Stand or sit with stillness. Breathe through your nose. Let others speak first. Let the room come to **you**. Men of presence don't react to the energy of the space—they **recalibrate it** with their calm.

If and when you do speak, do so with control, clarity, and minimal words. Let people adjust to your rhythm, not the other way around.

◆ 5. Your Energy is the Message

More than your words, more than your looks, people respond to your **energetic signature**.

- If you walk in rushed, needy, or apologetic, they feel it.

- If you walk in with tension or entitlement, they resist it.

- But if you walk in **grounded, focused, calm, and open**, they gravitate toward it—without knowing why.

This is the CEO effect. Not corporate, but **commanding**. Not performative, but **anchored**. Not attention-seeking, but **attention-commanding**.

Final Note: Be the Atmosphere, Not the Noise

When you walk into a room with presence, you're not just part of the environment—you become the **atmosphere** itself.

You shift the tempo. You alter the tone. You create a ripple just by entering.

That doesn't happen by trying harder. It happens by being **still enough, certain enough**, and **clear enough** to let your frame lead the way. Walk in like nothing needs to be said—because the room already heard you.

Reading the Room Like a Leader

A leader isn't defined by how loud they speak, but by how well they **listen**, **observe**, and **adapt** to the environment around them. The ability to "read the room" is more than just noticing what's said—it's understanding **what's not being said**, what **people are feeling**, and what the **underlying energy** of the space demands.

True masculine presence isn't just about leading with strength—it's about knowing when to amplify your energy and when to step back. It's about understanding **how your presence shifts** the room, and how you can use that understanding to influence without force.

Here's how you can cultivate the skill of reading a room with the precision and depth of a seasoned leader.

◆ 1. Develop Awareness: Your First Step to Influence

The first rule of leadership is **awareness**—and it starts with **you**. Before you can understand others, you must understand how your own energy, behavior, and actions are affecting the room. Leaders know that everything they do sends a signal—whether they mean it to or not.

- **Posture**: Are you standing tall, or slouched? Are you leaning in too eagerly, or holding a confident stance? Your body speaks before your words do.

- **Energy**: Are you feeling tense, impatient, or disconnected? Are you projecting calm authority, or are you simply reacting to the room's energy? Leaders ground themselves before they engage with others.

Before even opening your mouth, **check your inner state**. A centered, grounded leader creates the space for others to feel safe, understood, and in sync.

◆ 2. Pay Attention to Non-Verbal Cues

Words are just a small part of the communication equation. A true leader is always paying attention to **body language**, **facial expressions**, and **tone of voice**—these cues reveal far more than spoken words ever can.

- **Body language**: Are people crossing their arms, looking away, or leaning in? These micro-actions tell you whether people feel closed off, engaged, or uncertain. Leaders interpret these signals and adjust accordingly.

- **Facial expressions**: Subtle shifts in someone's face often reveal more about their feelings than they're willing to admit. A furrowed brow, a tight jaw, or a half-smile can indicate discomfort, skepticism, or curiosity. You need to spot these signs to adjust your approach.

- **Tone**: The way someone says something is as important as what they say. Are they speaking with confidence or hesitancy? Is their voice sharp, hesitant, or calm? A leader listens not just for content, but for **emotion** in their tone.

Being aware of these signals allows you to **adapt your approach** in real-time. If someone's body language is closed, for instance, you may choose to approach them with more openness or a calm demeanor to ease tension.

◆ 3. Tune into the Group's Energy

Every room, meeting, or gathering has its own **collective energy**—an undercurrent of emotion and vibe that exists beneath the surface. Leaders learn to **tune into this collective atmosphere** and adapt their approach accordingly.

- **Positive energy**: If the group feels energized, open, and confident, a leader can build on that momentum. They can speak with authority and guide the conversation to new heights.

- **Tension or uncertainty**: If there's underlying tension, a leader must recognize it and either diffuse it or redirect it. Silence, calm statements, and steady energy can often clear the air when discomfort or doubt fills the room.

- **Lack of engagement**: If people are disengaged, a leader knows how to reignite interest without forcing it. They may ask questions, share a relevant insight, or subtly challenge the group to think differently.

Reading the room is about **feeling the pulse** of the group and understanding when to push, when to pull back, and when to let things unfold naturally.

◆ 4. Adapt Your Approach Based on the Room's Needs

Once you've observed the energy, body language, and emotional atmosphere, it's time to adapt. A leader is a **chameleon**, able to shift his approach based on the needs of the moment.

- **Calm the storm**: In moments of chaos or high tension, the leader remains calm, composed, and focused. He adjusts his voice, energy, and communication style to guide the group toward clarity.

- **Step into the spotlight**: When the group needs direction or a clear decision, the leader steps forward, with clarity and confidence. He uses his body, voice, and presence to command attention and lead the way.

- **Draw people out**: If a room feels stagnant or passive, a leader asks the right questions, makes eye contact, and draws people into the conversation, encouraging participation and engagement.

Understanding when to **lead**, when to **step back**, and when to **engage the group** is key to mastering this skill. Great leaders aren't static—they're **fluid**, constantly adjusting to the needs of the environment.

◆ 5. Trust Your Intuition

Finally, the best leaders know how to trust their intuition. After reading the room's energy, body language, and tone, your gut will often give you the final **signal** on how to act. Leaders listen to their instincts, even when they don't have all the data or answers.

Your intuition is a reflection of your accumulated experiences, your understanding of human nature, and your awareness of the subtle dynamics at play. **Trust it.**

Whether it's noticing that someone's discomfort is rooted in something personal, or sensing that the room's energy needs a jolt of enthusiasm, a grounded leader learns to follow the quiet whispers of his inner knowing.

Final Note: Master the Silent Language of Leadership

Reading the room isn't just about **hearing** what's being said. It's about understanding the **unspoken language** of energy, emotions, and dynamics. As a leader, your ability to tune into these signals—whether positive or negative—gives you the power to influence the room without exerting force.

When you know how to **read** a room and adapt to its needs, you lead with more authority than anyone who simply commands. True masculine leadership isn't about dominating the space—it's about understanding it, owning it, and **shaping** it.

5

Assertive Calm – Dominance Without Aggression

Dominance vs. Domineering

Dominance, at its core, is about **leading** without force, creating an environment where others naturally gravitate toward your energy, direction, and decisions. It's a reflection of your internal strength and **grounded confidence**, not an attempt to impose your will on others.

A dominant man doesn't need to shout or make waves. His presence **speaks** for itself. He **sets the tone** of a room, not by making noise, but by simply embodying strength, clarity, and authority. Dominance is magnetic. It draws people in, not out of fear, but out of respect and trust.

Key qualities of dominance:

- **Clarity and decisiveness**: A dominant man makes decisions quickly and confidently, which creates a sense of safety and security in others. His certainty provides direction.

- **Self-containment**: He doesn't rely on external validation or approval to feel worthy. His sense of value comes from within.

- **Respect for others**: A dominant person respects other people's boundaries and autonomy. He leads through influence, not coercion.

- **Non-reactive presence**: He remains unshaken by external stimuli, which gives others the opportunity to act with calm themselves.

Dominance is not about needing to be **seen** or **heard** all the time. It's about creating an environment where your confidence and presence naturally influence the behavior of others. It's quiet power, not explosive force.

◆ Domineering: Forceful, Controlling, and Overbearing

In contrast, **domineering** behavior is the attempt to control others, often through overt aggression or manipulation. It stems from **insecurity**, a deep need to prove one's worth by dominating, manipulating, or imposing one's will on others. The domineering man is **driven by the fear of losing power** and therefore pushes constantly to assert himself over others, often in harmful or obnoxious ways.

Domineering is rooted in **external validation** and an obsessive need to make sure others recognize one's authority. It may appear forceful or assertive at first glance, but in reality, it comes from a place of deep inner **weakness**, fear, and lack of self-assurance.

Key qualities of domineering behavior:

- **Incessant control**: A domineering person needs to dictate everything—what people say, how they behave, where they go. His entire identity is wrapped up in **controlling the situation**.

- **Aggression**: Domineering individuals often resort to loudness, sarcasm, or even intimidation to maintain control. They aren't interested in healthy dialogue, but in silencing others.

- **Overstepping boundaries**: The domineering individual disregards others' needs and personal space, constantly pushing to exert their influence, regardless of the environment or context.

- **Defensiveness**: A domineering man becomes hostile or defensive when his authority is questioned. He fears that if others don't recognize his "power," he will lose it.

Unlike dominance, which attracts followers through trust and respect, **domineering** behavior pushes people away, creating a toxic environment of fear, resentment, and rebellion.

◆ **The Subtle Difference: How to Avoid Crossing the Line**

The line between **dominance** and **domineering** is often subtle. To stay on the right side, consider these practical approaches:

1. **Lead by example, not by force.** True dominance comes from embodying the traits you want to see in others. You don't need to force compliance; you just need to **model behavior** and set clear expectations. A domineering person demands respect—often through fear—while a dominant person **commands** respect through their own behavior.

2. **Be non-reactive, not controlling.** Reacting to every little thing shows insecurity. Dominance is about responding thoughtfully, not pushing others into submission. When you feel the urge to control the conversation or situation, pause and ask yourself if you are leading from a place of confidence or fear.

3. **Respect the space of others.** Dominance is about **guiding**, not about **taking over**. A true leader knows when to step back and allow others to shine. If you are consistently overshadowing others or forcing your opinions, you're not leading—you're dominating. Leadership is about **empowering**, not diminishing.

4. **Embrace silence over domination.** When you feel your authority slipping or your influence waning, resist the temptation to raise your voice or make your presence felt through dominance. Instead, become more **present**. **Silence** often amplifies your power, signaling control without exerting force.

Final Note: Dominance Comes from Within, Not Without

Dominance is the ability to **command** attention without **demanding** it. It's about embodying calm, grounded strength that influences and inspires others, not about making them bend to your will. A truly dominant man doesn't need to assert himself aggressively—his power speaks for itself in the way he holds space, in his ability to stay calm under pressure, and in his unwavering self-belief.

The domineering man, on the other hand, constantly **pushes**, **prods**, and **proves** himself, never trusting that his own natural energy is enough to draw respect. His need for validation makes him insecure, and his aggression alienates others.

By mastering the art of **assertive calm**, you can project your dominance without resorting to domineering tactics, ultimately leading with power, purpose, and integrity.

Calm Eyes, Controlled Posture

The eyes are often called the **windows to the soul**, but when it comes to cultivating a masculine frame, they also serve as windows to your inner strength, confidence, and resilience. Similarly, your posture—the way you carry yourself in the world—speaks volumes without uttering a single word. Together, your **calm eyes** and **controlled posture** form the foundation of a powerful, unshakable presence.

In this section, we'll explore how these two components of your physical presence can signal **inner strength**, **self-mastery**, and **stoic calm** to the world, and how you can refine them to develop a magnetic and grounded frame.

◆ **Calm Eyes: The Gateway to Inner Peace**

Your eyes communicate more than you might realize. A man who has cultivated true masculine presence knows that his gaze is not just a way to see the world—it's a **way to convey certainty**. In moments of tension or chaos, a calm, steady gaze can be the difference between **losing control** and **maintaining composure**.

A steady gaze doesn't need to be cold or disinterested—it should be calm, present, and open. It reflects the **depth of your inner peace** and the **clarity of your thoughts**. When you look at others with calm eyes, you project confidence, control, and **emotional regulation**, inviting others to trust you without saying a word.

The power of calm eyes:

- **Conveys confidence**: A calm, steady gaze reflects your **self-assurance**. It's the opposite of a nervous or jittery look, which signals discomfort and uncertainty.

- **Invites trust**: When you lock eyes with someone, a calm, grounded gaze signals that you are fully present, **focused**, and **unreactive**. People trust those who don't feel the need to look away or break eye contact out of insecurity.

- **Project emotional control**: In moments of challenge or stress, keeping your eyes calm and unfazed shows your ability to control your emotions, rather than be controlled by them.

To develop calm eyes:

- **Practice mindful eye contact**: When conversing with someone, maintain eye contact to show engagement and respect. Let your gaze be soft and unwavering. Avoid staring aggressively, but don't look away or dart your eyes nervously.

- **Visualize stillness**: When feeling anxious or uncertain, take a moment to focus on your breath and soften your gaze. Imagine your eyes as calm waters, reflecting the clarity and stillness of your mind.

- **Slow your blinking**: Rapid blinking can signal nervousness or stress. Practice slowing your blink rate, especially in moments when you want to project authority or control.

◆ **Controlled Posture: The Body as an Anchor**

Posture is more than just the way you stand—it's a reflection of your **mental state**, your **emotional regulation**, and your **level of presence**. A man who carries himself with **controlled posture** is a man who has mastered his inner world. The way you stand, sit, and move in space sends a powerful message to the world about how you see yourself—and how others should see you.

The foundation of controlled posture:

- **Neutrality over tension**: A strong, masculine posture is neutral—neither too rigid nor too relaxed. This is the posture of someone who is neither on edge nor slouching, but instead **anchored** in the present moment.

- **Space and presence**: Controlled posture doesn't just keep you upright—it also **expands** your presence. Standing tall with shoulders back gives the impression of strength and stability. This posture invites others to feel safe around you, without needing to dominate or intimidate.

- **Adaptability**: A well-controlled posture also allows for adaptability. A strong frame doesn't mean a **stiff** frame. A man who is grounded and present knows how to adjust his posture to suit the situation—sitting attentively in a meeting, standing with authority during a presentation, or relaxing with ease when appropriate.

To cultivate controlled posture:

- **Stand tall, but relaxed**: Imagine a string pulling you upward from the crown of your head, lengthening your spine without forcing it. Keep your shoulders relaxed, not tense. Your posture should convey openness, not defensiveness.

- **Move with purpose**: The way you move in space should mirror the same grounded, purposeful attitude. Avoid fidgeting or pacing unnecessarily. Walk slowly, deliberately, and with intention.

- **Root yourself**: When standing, ensure that your feet are firmly planted, with a slight bend in your knees. This will give you a sense of stability and control. When sitting, ensure your back is straight, and your body is well-aligned to avoid slouching.

- **Mirror the energy of the room**: A controlled posture doesn't mean you must be stiff or out of place. **Read the room** and adapt your posture to suit the situation, whether you're in a casual setting or an intense discussion. Still, always maintain a sense of grounded presence.

◆ The Connection Between Eyes and Posture

Your **eyes** and **posture** work together to create a unified message of grounded strength. One without the other can leave a gap in your presence. For example, a calm gaze paired with a slouched posture can seem passive or unsure, while a strong, upright posture with a jittery gaze may communicate tension rather than confidence.

Together, your eyes and posture should create a seamless **aura of control, composure**, and **clarity**. When both your eyes and your body reflect calmness, you become an unspoken pillar in the room—a silent yet powerful force that commands attention and inspires trust.

Final Note: A Stillness That Speaks Volumes

Mastering **calm eyes** and **controlled posture** is an act of embodied stoicism. It's not about projecting fake confidence—it's about connecting with the **inner stillness** that lies at the core of your being. When you become the embodiment of **calm strength** and **centeredness**, the world around you feels that energy. Your eyes communicate your inner peace, and your posture anchors you firmly in the present moment.

In moments of challenge, uncertainty, or tension, your calm eyes and controlled posture become your silent allies—reminding you that you are unshaken and unafraid. And when you move through the world with this level of presence, others naturally gravitate toward your grounded energy, instinctively trusting that you are a man who is **in control**, yet never overbearing.

Setting Boundaries with Subtle Force

Setting boundaries is one of the most powerful tools a man can develop in maintaining his masculine frame. The ability to set boundaries effectively—without being overtly aggressive or passive—requires a balance of **strength, clarity**, and **self-respect**. This is where **subtle force** comes in: the ability to assert your needs and limits in a way that is firm yet calm, confident yet compassionate.

Boundaries aren't about control; they're about creating a space where **respect**, **autonomy**, and **personal integrity** are upheld. By setting clear boundaries with subtle force, you teach others how to treat you while maintaining an unwavering composure. You don't have to yell, manipulate, or create drama. Instead, you **simply embody** the unspoken message: "This is who I am, and this is what I accept."

In this section, we'll explore how to set boundaries with strength and subtlety, ensuring that your frame remains intact without crossing the line into aggression or submission.

◆ The Nature of Boundaries: A Foundation of Self-Respect

Boundaries are the invisible lines that define where **you** end and others begin. They are essential in protecting your time, energy, emotional well-being, and physical space. The act of setting boundaries isn't just about saying "no" or creating distance; it's about communicating clearly and firmly that you **value yourself** and that your needs are important.

When you lack boundaries, you're essentially allowing others to impose on your energy, time, and resources, often to your detriment. Without boundaries, you lose **control** over how you spend your time, how you engage with people, and ultimately, how you show up in the world.

When you set boundaries with **subtle force**, you create an environment in which you are **respected**, **valued**, and **able to thrive**. The key to setting boundaries without conflict lies in the ability to do so with calm authority and a deep understanding of your own worth.

◆ The Power of Calm Assertion

The essence of **subtle force** is rooted in **calm assertion**—the ability to express your needs and boundaries in a way that is firm yet gentle, clear yet open. Assertiveness is not about being demanding or rude; it's about being

unwavering in your clarity. When you assert your boundaries, it's not about a power struggle; it's about ensuring that your needs are met in a manner that does not require over-explanation or apology.

A man who uses subtle force to set boundaries is not only clear about what he wants but also **detached** from any emotional charge. He doesn't allow others' reactions to dictate his sense of self-worth. Whether someone agrees with your boundary or not, the act of calmly asserting it is a reflection of **self-respect**, not a desire for approval.

Examples of calm assertion in setting boundaries:

- "I can't engage with this conversation right now, but I'm happy to talk later."

- "I respect your opinion, but I have a different perspective, and I'd like to stick with that."

- "I value my time and prefer not to have my schedule disrupted."

In each of these examples, the boundary is clear, and the tone remains calm and respectful. There's no hesitation, no apology, just a firm statement of **self-worth**.

◆ Body Language and Energy in Boundary Setting

Your **body language** and **energy** play a crucial role in setting boundaries with subtle force. Non-verbal communication often conveys more than words ever can. When you set a boundary, your **physical presence** should align with the message you are delivering.

- **Posture**: Stand tall, but relaxed. Your posture should convey that you are centered and grounded, which reinforces your words without needing to be forceful.

- **Eye contact**: Maintain calm and steady eye contact. Looking someone directly in the eyes communicates confidence, control, and an unwavering sense of self-respect.

- **Voice**: Your voice should be clear, calm, and steady, not wavering or apologetic. Speaking with a deep, firm tone reinforces the strength of your boundary and shows that it's non-negotiable.

In essence, your body and energy should **align with your words**, creating an environment where the boundary is respected without the need for confrontation.

◆ **Handling Pushback with Grace**

Inevitably, when you set boundaries, you may face **pushback**—whether from people who are used to taking more of your time or energy, or from those who are uncomfortable with the change. The key here is to remain **unmoved**, not through stubbornness, but through a deep sense of calm resolve.

You must remember that **pushback is not a reflection of your worth**; it's simply a test of your commitment to your own boundaries. Your ability to stand firm without engaging in emotional drama is the hallmark of a man who uses **subtle force** to maintain his integrity.

When faced with pushback, avoid:

- Over-explaining your boundary

- Apologizing for asserting your needs

- Becoming defensive or reactive

Instead, respond with a calm, brief statement that reinforces your boundary and shifts the focus back to **your self-respect**.

Examples of handling pushback:

- "I understand you may feel differently, but this is important to me, and I'm not willing to compromise."

- "I'm happy to discuss this another time, but I can't engage right now."

- "I hear your concerns, but I've made my decision and stand by it."

This response is simple, clear, and non-reactive. It signals that your boundaries are not up for negotiation, while also maintaining the **peaceful authority** that defines your masculine frame.

◆ **The Subtle Force of Saying "No"**

One of the most powerful uses of subtle force in boundary setting is the ability to say **"no"** without guilt or explanation. Many men struggle with saying no because they fear disappointing others, being perceived as rude, or damaging relationships. But the truth is that **saying no** is an act of self-respect, not selfishness.

A strong man knows that he **cannot say yes** to everything without sacrificing his time, energy, and focus. By saying no when necessary, you create space for what truly matters—your goals, values, and personal well-being.

- **Say no when necessary**: Don't be afraid to say no if a request doesn't align with your priorities or boundaries.

- **Say no without guilt**: You don't need to apologize for protecting your time and energy. Saying no is simply a reflection of your **self-respect**.

- **Be firm, not defensive**: Don't make excuses or offer lengthy explanations. A simple, direct "no" is often the most powerful response.

Final Note: Boundaries Are a Sign of Inner Strength

Setting boundaries with subtle force is an art that requires clarity, confidence, and self-awareness. It's about knowing **who you are**, **what you need**, and **what you will not tolerate**. When you set your boundaries calmly and assertively, you send a message to the world that you are **strong, grounded**, and **in control** of your life.

In a world that often pushes people to overextend themselves, setting clear and firm boundaries with subtle force is one of the most powerful ways you can maintain your masculine frame and honor your integrity. It's a demonstration of respect—respect for yourself and others—and a critical skill for anyone who wants to live a life of **purpose, clarity**, and **power**.

Learning to Take Up Space (Physically and Socially)

One of the most powerful expressions of masculine frame is the ability to take up space—both physically and socially. It's an act of claiming your presence, your value, and your right to exist fully in any room you enter. When you take up space, you signal to the world that you are grounded, confident, and comfortable in your own skin.

This doesn't mean taking over or dominating others; rather, it's about owning your energy and showing up as your authentic self without shrinking or apologizing for your existence. The ability to take up space is a reflection of your inner strength—your ability to be present and unapologetic about your place in the world.

In this section, we will explore what it means to take up space physically and socially, and how to cultivate this powerful trait to enhance your masculine frame.

◆ The Power of Physical Presence

Physically taking up space is an expression of confidence. It involves how you stand, how you move, and how you carry yourself through the world. A man who takes up space is not timid or hunched over; he stands tall, takes a solid stance, and moves with intention.

Your body is a powerful communicator of your internal state. When you take up space physically, you signal to others that you are grounded, that you belong, and that you will not shrink in the face of challenges.

Key aspects of physical space:

- Posture: Stand tall, with your chest open, shoulders back, and your head held high. Imagine a string pulling you upwards from the top of your head, elongating your spine and creating an aura of strength and confidence. A man who takes up space physically exudes a sense of presence that others can't ignore.

- Gestures: Use deliberate, controlled gestures that complement your grounded posture. Avoid fidgeting, crossing your arms defensively, or shrinking into yourself. When you gesture, let it be with intention—your movements should mirror your calm authority.

- Space between you and others: Don't apologize for the space you occupy. When you stand or sit, don't crowd others unnecessarily, but also don't make yourself small. Allow yourself to spread out, take up room, and own your physical presence.

Taking up space physically is about confidence in your own body. The more you do this, the more comfortable you will become in your own skin, and the more others will feel the subtle power that radiates from you.

◆ Social Presence: Owning Your Place in Any Room

Taking up space socially is just as important as taking up space physically. It involves claiming your voice, your opinion, and your right to engage authentically in social settings without shrinking into the background or relying on others to dictate your participation.

A man who takes up social space does not wait for permission to be heard. He engages in conversations with clarity, purpose, and confidence, knowing that his voice and presence are valuable.

Key aspects of social space:

- Voice and presence: Speak with clarity, depth, and conviction. Your voice should be measured, not overly loud, but deep enough to command attention without demanding it. A man who owns his social space doesn't need to dominate the conversation, but his words carry weight and authority.

- Engagement: Take the initiative to contribute to discussions. Whether in a meeting, a group of friends, or a social gathering, show up and make your thoughts known. A man who takes up space socially engages others in meaningful ways, instead of fading into the background.

- Emotional presence: When you take up space socially, it's not just about your physical presence or words—it's about being fully present in the moment. Your energy, attention, and emotional investment in conversations signal that you are invested, engaged, and authentic.

To take up space socially, you need to be comfortable with the idea that your presence is worthy of attention. Let go of the need to seek approval or validation and learn to show up fully in every situation.

The Psychology of Taking Up Space

Taking up space, both physically and socially, is rooted in the psychology of self-worth and self-acceptance. When you take up space, you are essentially telling the world that you believe you have a right to exist, and that you are worthy of being seen and heard.

In a world that often encourages people to shrink, be modest, or fade into the background, taking up space requires a level of bravery and self-assurance. It's a declaration that you are enough just as you are—and that your presence is a gift to those around you.

When you take up space, you stop seeking permission to exist and start owning your impact on the world. Whether in personal relationships, professional settings, or social situations, your presence should communicate that you are fully here, fully engaged, and worthy of respect.

Overcoming the Fear of Being Too Much

Many men struggle with the fear of being "too much" when they take up space. This fear often stems from conditioning—society tells us to be humble, to avoid standing out, and to take up as little space as possible to keep things comfortable for others. But this conditioning is a trap that robs you of your full potential.

Taking up space is not about arrogance or seeking attention for the sake of attention—it's about owning your right to exist and showing up in the world as your true self. When you embrace this, you'll find that the fear of being "too much" fades away, replaced with the confidence that you are just enough.

Start small, and gradually allow yourself to expand in both physical and social spaces. This could mean taking a more prominent seat at the table, voicing your opinion more frequently, or simply standing a little taller in any room you enter. With practice, you'll realize that you're not taking up too much space—you're simply taking up the space that is rightfully yours.

◆ The Impact of Taking Up Space

When you learn to take up space, you become a magnetic presence in any room. People are drawn to your confidence, your self-assuredness, and your clarity of purpose. You stop waiting for validation from others, and instead, you create an energy that attracts respect, trust, and admiration.

Taking up space is also a sign of leadership. People look to those who are comfortable with their own presence for guidance. When you take up space, you inspire others to do the same, creating a ripple effect of empowerment and authenticity.

The world needs men who are confident enough to own their presence, to stand tall, and to show up as their true selves. When you take up space, you contribute not only to your own growth but to the growth of everyone around you.

Final Note: Stand Tall and Be Seen

Learning to take up space—physically and socially—is about honoring your worth and owning your place in the world. It requires bravery, self-acceptance, and a willingness to show up as the best version of yourself, unapologetically and without hesitation. When you take up space, you claim your right to be seen, heard, and respected, and in doing so, you transform your world.

In mastering the art of taking up space, you cultivate a frame that is magnetic, resilient, and unshakable—and you begin to lead with quiet strength, drawing others into your orbit with the power of your presence.

6

Earning Command - Authority

How Authority is Perceived and Given

Authority is often misunderstood. Many people think that authority is something you claim or demand through force or loud declarations, but true authority is something far more subtle—and more powerful. It is earned, not imposed. It is not a title, but a **presence**. It is not about exerting power over others; it's about becoming someone whose **words**, **actions**, and **energy** naturally command respect.

In this section, we will explore how authority is perceived by others, how it is cultivated through character, and how you can earn and solidify your command over any situation.

◆ Authority is an Energy, Not Just a Title

Authority doesn't come from a position, a title, or the number of people who report to you. While positions of power might give you a platform, true authority is about how others **perceive** you—not just based on what you say, but how you make them feel.

True authority is an energy, a **quiet command** that doesn't need to be shouted from the rooftops. People with genuine authority don't demand attention or approval; their mere **presence** and **confidence** ensure they are noticed. They don't chase respect—they **attract it**. Their very being radiates the message, "I know who I am, and I know what I stand for."

When you walk into a room, your authority is **felt** before it is acknowledged. It doesn't require force or boasting. Instead, it is a subtle but undeniable **magnetism** that commands the focus and respect of others.

◆ **The Building Blocks of Perceived Authority**

People perceive authority through a combination of **presence**, **actions**, and **words**. Your authority is shaped by how you behave, how you communicate, and how others experience you over time.

Here are the primary building blocks that help form your perceived authority:

1. **Consistency**: Authority is built through **reliability** and **predictability**. When you are consistent in your actions and behaviors, people start to trust that you are someone who can be counted on. They begin to recognize you as a person of **integrity** and **stability**.

2. **Competence**: True authority is earned through **mastery** and **skill**. Whether it's in your professional life, personal relationships, or any area of your expertise, demonstrating your **proficiency** and **knowledge** gives you the **credibility** that others will naturally respect. A man with authority knows what he's talking about and has the competence to back it up.

3. **Confidence**: People perceive authority in those who carry themselves with **confidence**—not arrogance, but a **quiet assurance** that comes from knowing your worth and abilities. This confidence instills trust and cultivates a sense of leadership. When you speak or act with conviction, others will naturally follow your lead.

4. **Emotional Control**: Authority is not about being emotionally volatile or reactive. Rather, it's about maintaining **poise** in any situation. When you demonstrate calm and composed behavior, especially under pressure, you display the kind of emotional **intelligence** that others look to in leaders.

5. **Clear Communication**: A person who can communicate clearly, with purpose, and without hesitation instantly earns authority. When you speak with **clarity** and **decisiveness**, people listen. They respect those who can articulate their thoughts effectively and present them with **confidence**.

◆ Authority is Earned, Not Demanded

While some may be tempted to **demand** authority through force, the truth is that authority is something that must be earned over time. It is the result of how you conduct yourself, how you treat others, and how you **lead** by example.

Demanding authority often leads to **resistance** and resentment. People don't respond to aggression or coercion; they respond to **authenticity** and **respect**. Real authority doesn't need to be shouted—it is **quietly earned** through consistent actions that align with your values, integrity, and vision.

The process of earning authority involves **demonstrating your capabilities**, **staying true to your word**, and **being a person of high character**. It's about leading with **wisdom**, not just power, and cultivating relationships built on **mutual respect**. Over time, others will see your authority as something natural, something that cannot be questioned.

◆ How Authority is Given by Others

While you may cultivate your authority, it is ultimately **given to you** by those around you. People choose to respect you based on how they perceive your actions, your integrity, and your ability to guide or lead them.

Trust is at the heart of giving authority. For others to **acknowledge** your authority, they must trust you. Trust is earned when you consistently prove that you have their best interests in mind, that you lead with **clarity**, and that you act in a way that aligns with your words.

In essence, authority is a **social contract**. It's an exchange of respect and trust. You demonstrate your ability to lead, guide, and support others, and in return, they give you their **allegiance**, **attention**, and **respect**. The more you demonstrate your ability to add value to others, the more **authority** they will place in you.

◆ The Role of Boundaries in Authority

One of the key aspects of maintaining authority is the ability to **set and enforce boundaries**. Strong boundaries signal that you have **self-respect**, and that you expect the same from others. By enforcing healthy boundaries, you reinforce the idea that you are a person who stands by his principles and does not tolerate disrespect or manipulation.

When you set boundaries with **firmness** and **grace**, you are asserting your authority without the need for aggression. You show that you are **in control** of your time, energy, and emotional well-being. This in turn strengthens your leadership and the respect others have for you.

◆ Leading Through Influence, Not Force

True authority is about **influence**, not force. It's about guiding others through **vision, wisdom,** and **empathy**—not through control or coercion. As you earn your authority, you begin to **influence** those around you, not by demanding obedience, but by inspiring it.

When you lead with authority, others don't just follow because they have to— they follow because they **want to**. They see in you a leader who can **guide them**, someone who **stands firm in his values**, and someone whose presence inspires trust and respect.

Final Thoughts: Becoming a True Authority

To earn command and authority is to become a **pillar of strength, integrity,** and **purpose**. It is about **consistency, competence,** and **clarity**. True authority isn't something you claim—it's something you cultivate by living in alignment with your values, leading by example, and earning the respect of those around you.

As you continue to build your masculine frame, remember that **authority is a reflection of your true self**. It comes from being grounded in your purpose, treating others with respect, and being confident in your own skin. **Authority is**

given to you by those who recognize your **presence**, your **impact**, and the **integrity** you bring to everything you do.

Speaking with Conviction

In the world of masculine frame, **speaking with conviction** is not just about what you say; it's about how you say it. The ability to speak confidently, decisively, and with clear purpose is one of the most powerful tools at your disposal for commanding respect and authority.

When you speak with conviction, you make a statement—not just with your words but with the **force** behind them. People instinctively respect individuals who speak with belief in their message, because it signals certainty, authenticity, and a **deep understanding** of their subject. Your words carry weight, and they invite others to listen, reflect, and engage with you in a meaningful way.

In this section, we'll break down how to cultivate the ability to speak with conviction—transforming your communication into an expression of true **authority** and **influence**.

- **The Power of Certainty**

Conviction begins with **certainty**. When you speak with certainty, you make it clear that you are not just offering an opinion—you are presenting a **truth** that you deeply believe in. Certainty is contagious. When others sense that you are resolute in your words, they are more likely to trust your perspective, follow your lead, and take action based on your guidance.

To speak with conviction, you must first **believe in what you are saying**. Whether you are discussing your ideas, offering advice, or giving instructions, certainty comes from knowing your subject matter inside and out. If you lack knowledge or clarity on a topic, it will be harder to project conviction because the **confidence** needed to speak with authority will be missing.

Key tips to develop certainty in your speech:

- **Be prepared**: Know your material or point of view before you speak. Do your research and understand the core of what you are communicating.

- **Believe in your message**: Even if you are speaking about something that's challenging or outside your comfort zone, approach it with the mindset that your perspective has value.

- **Trust your intuition**: Sometimes conviction comes not just from logical understanding but from **inner belief**. Trust that your instincts are valuable and let them guide your words.

◆ The Tone of Your Voice

The way you use your voice plays a significant role in conveying conviction. **Tone** is often more powerful than the words themselves. When you speak with authority, your voice should carry a certain **depth** and **resonance**. A voice that's shaky or hesitant diminishes your perceived confidence, while a strong, steady tone commands attention.

To speak with conviction, focus on the following aspects of your vocal delivery:

- **Volume**: Speaking too softly can make you seem uncertain, while speaking too loudly can appear forceful or aggressive. The key is a steady volume that matches the importance of your message. A well-timed **increase in volume** can help emphasize key points.

- **Pacing**: Speaking too quickly can suggest nervousness or a lack of preparation. Speaking too slowly may come across as unsure or unconfident. Find a comfortable **pace** that allows your words to land with impact. Pauses, when used strategically, can heighten the effect of what you're saying.

- **Pitch**: A deep, steady pitch often conveys authority, while a higher pitch can sometimes signal nervousness or uncertainty. Focus on **lowering** your natural pitch slightly when speaking to add weight to your words.

◆ Body Language That Reinforces Your Words

Your words can have immense power, but they must be backed up by your body language. When speaking with conviction, your **body** needs to support your message. The way you hold yourself while speaking sends an even stronger signal than the words you use. Conviction is conveyed not just through speech but through your **presence**.

Here's how to align your body language with the authority you want to communicate:

- **Posture**: Stand or sit with your back straight, shoulders open, and head held high. A strong posture naturally projects confidence and makes your words feel more impactful.

- **Gestures**: Use purposeful, deliberate gestures to underscore your points. Don't fidget or make nervous movements. Your hands should move naturally and in harmony with your speech, but not too much. Controlled gestures add emphasis without distracting from your words.

- **Eye contact**: When you speak, maintain strong but comfortable **eye contact** with your audience. This helps convey that you are not only confident in your words but also engaged with those you are speaking to. It also signals that you are unafraid to be seen and heard.

◆ The Importance of Clarity and Brevity

Speaking with conviction also requires that you are **clear** and **concise** in your message. A person who speaks confidently often doesn't need to say much—they know that fewer, more powerful words will leave a lasting impression.

When you speak with conviction, avoid **over-explaining** or overloading your audience with information. Keep your message **simple**, **direct**, and to the point. People appreciate clarity because it makes your message **memorable** and **easy to understand**.

To improve your clarity and brevity:

- **Simplify your thoughts**: Focus on distilling your message to its core essence. Avoid unnecessary details or tangents that might dilute your point.

- **Eliminate filler words**: Words like "um," "uh," and "like" undermine your conviction. Practice speaking without these fillers, and allow yourself to pause for a moment instead of using empty words to fill space.

- **Be intentional with every word**: Each word you speak should serve a purpose. Avoid rambling or hedging your language with uncertainty.

◆ **Overcoming Doubt and Fear of Rejection**

One of the greatest obstacles to speaking with conviction is the **fear of being wrong** or the fear of rejection. Many people hesitate to speak with full authority because they worry others will disagree with them, or they doubt their own opinions and knowledge.

To overcome this fear, remember that conviction doesn't require you to be infallible—it requires you to **believe in what you're saying** and to communicate it **assertively**. Confidence doesn't mean you're always right; it means you **stand by your words**, regardless of external validation.

To overcome doubt:

- **Practice self-assurance**: Remind yourself that your ideas, opinions, and perspectives have value, even if they are challenged. Confidence comes from within.

- **Accept disagreement**: Not everyone will agree with you, and that's okay. True conviction means standing strong even in the face of opposition, without losing composure or authority.

- **Reframe failure**: Instead of fearing rejection or being wrong, view it as an opportunity for growth. People respect those who can maintain their composure even when challenged.

Final Thoughts: Speaking with Purpose

To speak with conviction is to **speak with purpose**. It's not about dominating the conversation but about presenting your **truth** in a way that **compels** others to listen and engage. By speaking clearly, confidently, and with intent, you signal to the world that your voice matters, your opinions have weight, and your words have power.

As you cultivate this skill, you'll find that your ability to command respect and authority grows exponentially. Speaking with conviction becomes a natural extension of your **masculine frame**, empowering you to lead, influence, and inspire others through the quiet power of your voice.

Creating Behavioral Consistency

In the realm of masculine frame and authority, there is one trait that acts as a **foundation** for everything else: **behavioral consistency**. It is the thread that weaves together the various aspects of your character—your strength, your power, your leadership—and makes them reliable, credible, and trustworthy in the eyes of others.

Behavioral consistency means that how you act, speak, and carry yourself aligns consistently with your core values, principles, and goals. It's about **predictability** in a world that's constantly shifting and unpredictable. When people encounter you, they know that your actions will match your words, and your words will reflect your thoughts.

This consistency doesn't just build trust—it also builds the **subtle authority** that comes from knowing that someone who acts with integrity, conviction, and reliability is someone who can be depended on to lead, guide, and protect.

In this section, we will explore why **behavioral consistency** is critical to your command and authority and how you can create it in your own life.

◆ Why Consistency is Key to Earning Respect

Behavioral consistency is one of the quickest ways to earn respect. People admire those who are **steady** in their approach, who don't waver or flip-flop depending on the situation or the people they're around. When you are consistent, others know what to expect from you, and this predictability fosters a sense of **safety** and **trust**.

Inconsistent behavior—being one way in private and another in public, or shifting your opinions to suit the crowd—sows doubt and undermines your credibility. When you act unpredictably, people become unsure of your intentions, and this **diminishes your authority**. Authority isn't just about projecting power—it's about being **reliable**. And being reliable requires consistency.

◆ The Impact of Consistency on Leadership

When you lead with **behavioral consistency**, you set the standard for those who follow you. Leaders who are consistent in their values, actions, and expectations create an environment where others feel secure and know exactly what to expect.

- **Predictable Leadership**: Your team, friends, or colleagues know how you'll react to certain situations. They know that if they need your guidance, your response will be **steady** and **measured**, and not influenced by emotion or external pressures.

- **Building Trust**: People place their trust in individuals who are **reliable** and **steadfast**. When you make decisions that align with your principles over time, you build a reputation for **integrity** and **sound judgment**, two qualities that are essential for strong leadership.

- **Strength Through Stability**: Consistent behavior provides emotional stability for those who look to you for direction. They find comfort in knowing that, no matter what happens, you will maintain a grounded, composed demeanor. This helps to create a sense of safety, allowing others to feel **empowered** under your leadership.

◆ How to Create Consistency in Your Actions

Creating behavioral consistency isn't just about making a few adjustments to how you act in public—it's about ensuring that your behavior is **aligned** with your core beliefs and principles in all areas of your life. Here are a few practical steps to help you maintain consistency:

1. **Clarify Your Core Values**: Before you can act consistently, you need to understand what you truly value. What principles guide you? What does **integrity** look like to you? Make a list of the values that you want to shape your actions, and ensure that these values inform every decision you make.

2. **Practice Self-Discipline**: Consistency requires a **high level of self-discipline**. This means sticking to your commitments, following through on your word, and doing what needs to be done even when it's difficult. The more you practice self-discipline, the easier it becomes to act in alignment with your values, even when challenges arise.

3. **Develop Routines**: Creating behavioral consistency starts with creating **routines** that support the traits you want to embody. For example, if you want to consistently project **calm confidence**, develop habits like meditation, journaling, or physical exercise to ground yourself before engaging in challenging conversations. Consistent behaviors, even small ones, build up over time to create a larger pattern of reliability.

4. **Follow Through on Commitments**: One of the quickest ways to build consistency is by simply following through on your promises. If you say you will do something, **do it**. This builds trust with others and shows that you are a man of your word. Consistent follow-through is essential for both personal and professional credibility.

5. **Reflect and Adjust**: Consistency doesn't mean rigidity. It's important to **reflect** on your actions regularly and ensure they're aligned with your values. If you find yourself acting inconsistently, take the time to reassess and make the necessary adjustments. Behavioral consistency is a long-term process, and self-awareness is key.

◆ How Consistency Cultivates Inner Confidence

When your behavior aligns with your values, you start to experience a **sense of congruence**—your thoughts, words, and actions are in harmony. This harmony creates a deep sense of inner **confidence**, because you no longer need to worry about whether you're projecting authenticity or whether your behavior is aligned with your true self.

You can move through life with **less internal conflict** because you are acting in alignment with who you are, which frees up mental and emotional energy. This **calm confidence** flows outward and is noticed by others, reinforcing your authority and **magnetic masculinity**.

◆ Avoiding Inconsistent Behavior: The Pitfalls to Watch Out For

While creating behavioral consistency is essential, there are some common pitfalls to be aware of. These can undermine your authority and erode trust:

1. **Being Driven by External Validation**: When your actions are constantly swayed by external opinions or the desire for approval, you lose the consistency that builds authority. Stay true to your principles, even when others challenge you or try to sway your beliefs.

2. **Changing Your Personality Based on the Situation**: It's important to adapt to different environments, but it's equally important that you don't morph into a completely different version of yourself to please others. People respect those who can **stay grounded** and true to themselves, no matter the context.

3. **Avoiding Difficult Conversations**: A lack of consistency can also come from avoiding the uncomfortable but necessary conversations that challenge the status quo. Failing to address problems or avoid confrontation for the sake of peace undermines your authority and leaves others questioning your commitment to your principles.

Final Thoughts: The Strength of Steady Leadership

Behavioral consistency is the invisible force that underpins true authority. When you act with integrity, follow through on your commitments, and stay true to your values, you become a rock for those around you. **Consistency** breeds **respect**, **trust**, and **command**. It gives you the **inner confidence** to lead effectively, inspire others, and **shape the world** around you with strength and clarity.

The more you align your actions with your core values, the more you'll find that **true leadership** comes naturally. Over time, your authority will become an extension of your consistency—something that others will admire and rely on.

Commanding Respect Without Demanding It

One of the most powerful aspects of masculine frame is the ability to command respect without ever having to **demand** it. True authority is not established through force or intimidation; rather, it is cultivated through consistency, integrity, and self-assuredness. When you embody these qualities, respect follows naturally, as a result of your presence, actions, and leadership.

Demanding respect often comes from a place of insecurity—an attempt to control others through fear or forceful behavior. This may bring temporary submission, but it doesn't create genuine **respect**. In contrast, those who command respect naturally do so by living in alignment with their values, demonstrating competence, and offering a sense of stability and confidence that others find compelling.

In this section, we will explore how to **command respect effortlessly**, the key traits that make it happen, and why people are more inclined to respect you when you don't have to demand it.

◆ The Subtle Power of Presence

Respect begins with your **presence**. When you walk into a room, your energy should speak louder than your words. People subconsciously gauge others based on their **energy**—whether it is calm and confident or chaotic and insecure. If you've developed a strong, masculine frame, your mere presence will command respect without you needing to say a word.

A calm, grounded presence makes it clear that you are not someone to be trifled with. There's no need to posture, brag, or assert dominance. People naturally sense that you have **control** over yourself and your environment, and this inspires respect.

To cultivate this presence:

- **Embody calmness**: Master the art of staying composed, even in high-pressure situations. This signals that you are unshaken by external circumstances, and others will respect you for your ability to maintain control.

- **Own your space**: Take up physical space in a room without being arrogant or overbearing. Stand tall, shoulders back, and make eye contact, allowing your body language to express confidence and assuredness.

◆ The Power of Consistency and Integrity

Respect is not something you can demand—it must be **earned** over time. One of the most effective ways to earn respect is by being **consistent** and **integral** in your actions. People are drawn to those who are dependable and aligned with their values. When your behavior and words match your core principles, others naturally begin to respect you.

Here's why:

- **Consistency builds trust**: Trust is at the foundation of respect. When you consistently follow through on your promises, act with integrity, and show up as the same person day after day, others know they can count on you.

- **Integrity commands admiration**: Integrity is about doing what is right, even when no one is watching. When people witness your unwavering commitment to doing the right thing, even in difficult situations, they will respect you for your moral courage.

◆ Setting Boundaries Without Aggression

One of the key components of commanding respect without demanding it is the ability to **set boundaries** clearly and firmly. Boundaries are not a form of aggression; they are a reflection of your self-respect and a way to communicate your needs and limits to others. People respect individuals who know where they stand and who aren't afraid to protect their time, energy, and values.

Setting boundaries is a subtle art:

- **Be clear but calm**: State your boundaries in a **firm, calm** manner. There is no need for drama or confrontation. Simply express what is acceptable and what isn't. Your clarity alone commands respect.

- **Stick to your boundaries**: The most important aspect of boundary-setting is **consistency**. If you set a boundary and allow others to violate it repeatedly, you'll lose respect in the process. Stand by your principles and maintain your boundaries with calm resolve.

◆ Leading by Example

Another key trait of commanding respect without demanding it is **leading by example**. The most powerful leaders don't have to force respect—they inspire it through their own actions. By consistently **modeling** the behaviors you expect from others, you set a standard that others are naturally inclined to follow.

When you live by the values you preach, when you work as hard as you expect others to work, and when you treat others with dignity and respect, you earn theirs in return.

Leading by example is one of the most powerful tools for gaining respect:

- **Be the embodiment of your principles**: Whether it's hard work, integrity, kindness, or discipline, your actions should reflect the standards you hold for others.

- **Empower others**: True leaders empower those around them by creating an environment where people can thrive. When you give others the opportunity to shine and lead, it creates a cycle of respect and admiration.

◆ The Trap of Seeking Approval

One of the most subtle ways in which people fail to command respect is by constantly seeking **approval** from others. When you need the validation of others to feel secure, you relinquish control over your own sense of self-worth. People can sense neediness, and it diminishes your authority. If you are constantly seeking approval or trying to appease others, you undermine the very respect you're trying to earn.

Respect comes from a place of **self-assurance**. It's about knowing your own value without needing others to constantly affirm it. When you speak, act, and lead without needing approval, others respect you for your authenticity and strength.

To avoid seeking approval:

- **Trust your judgment**: Stand firm in your decisions and opinions, even when they're not popular. The more you trust yourself, the more others will trust you.

- **Be secure in who you are**: Your self-worth should not depend on external validation. When you cultivate inner confidence, the need for approval fades, and true respect follows.

◆ The True Nature of Authority

When you command respect without demanding it, you are embodying true authority. **Authority** comes from within—it's the natural byproduct of a man who is calm, grounded, and aligned with his values. It is not about exerting power over others; it's about creating an environment where your influence is so undeniable that respect is given freely.

People don't respect authority because it's forced upon them; they respect it because it's earned through consistent, authentic actions. By living in alignment with your highest values and standards, you allow your presence to naturally command respect, without ever needing to demand it.

Final Thoughts: Leading with Quiet Strength

True masculine power is not about shouting for attention or forcing your will upon others. It's about leading with **quiet strength**—setting the standard through your actions, living with integrity, and remaining steadfast in your principles. When you lead with this kind of strength, respect comes as a natural byproduct.

Commanding respect without demanding it means embodying the very qualities you want others to admire. It means being the person who others look up to—not because you've forced them to, but because you've earned it through consistent, genuine behavior.

As you continue to develop your masculine frame, remember: The greatest leaders don't need to demand respect—they simply **earn it** through the power of their presence, their consistency, and their commitment to living a life of purpose and principle.

7

Substance Over Style - Gravitas

What It Means to Have Weight

Gravitas is one of the most elusive and powerful qualities that a man can possess. Unlike charm, charisma, or the more outward-facing aspects of masculine frame, gravitas operates on a deeper, more intrinsic level. It is the quiet strength that emanates from within, commanding the respect of others without the need for external validation. **Gravitas** is substance over style, depth over flash, and stability over showmanship. It's not something you can fake or fabricate—it is built through years of consistent action, integrity, and self-mastery.

In a world that often prioritizes the **loudest voice** or the **flashiest persona**, gravitas is the rare quality that transcends superficiality and connects directly to a person's **inner strength** and **moral foundation**. It's what makes someone stand out not because they're trying to be noticed, but because their presence is so powerful that it demands attention.

In this section, we'll explore how gravitas shapes your ability to command respect, the silent power it carries, and how you can cultivate this essential trait in your life.

◆ **What Is Gravitas?**

Gravitas can be described as the **weight of one's character**—it's the **depth** and **seriousness** of a man's presence that commands attention without needing to shout for it. When you have gravitas, people listen when you speak, and they pay attention when you enter a room, because they sense that your presence holds meaning. It's the quiet assurance that comes from being rooted in your principles, being wise in your decisions, and showing up with **consistent strength**.

Gravitas is not about being overly serious or distant; rather, it is about **self-possession**. It's about exuding the kind of inner confidence that assures others you have both the **competence** and the **moral grounding** to lead them. Those with gravitas have a way of commanding the moment without trying to dominate it. They make their presence felt through **subtle** and **steadfast** actions, not through noise or drama.

◆ Why Gravitas Matters

Gravitas is the quality that separates **leaders from followers**, the **respected** from the **admired**. It's the trait that creates trust in a leader's judgment, inspires loyalty, and makes people want to follow you—not because they feel obligated, but because they believe in your strength and wisdom. Without gravitas, even the most charismatic person can struggle to be taken seriously. But with it, even the most reserved or understated individual can become a **powerful force** of influence.

Here's why gravitas is crucial:

- **Elicits Trust**: Gravitas is rooted in **credibility**. It's the signal to others that you've seen the world and have the experience, wisdom, and foresight to navigate it. People follow those they trust, and gravitas builds that trust over time.

- **Instils Confidence**: When you have gravitas, you inspire confidence in others. You're not swayed by the crowd or subject to fleeting emotions. Your steady presence reassures people and gives them the courage to act.

- **Commands Respect**: Gravitas operates on a level that **demands respect** without having to ask for it. It's the internal weight you carry, your grounding in your own self-worth, that causes others to acknowledge and respect you.

◆ How to Develop Gravitas

Cultivating gravitas is a long-term process that requires **intentional** effort, discipline, and self-awareness. It's not about adopting a specific style or persona; it's about deepening your character, aligning your actions with your values, and learning to stand firm in your principles, no matter the circumstances.

Here are some actionable steps to help you develop gravitas:

1. **Cultivate Emotional Mastery**

   o Gravitas comes from a place of inner calm and emotional control. Learn to navigate your emotions, particularly in stressful or high-pressure situations. Practice mindfulness or meditation to keep your mind clear and your reactions measured.

   o When you control your emotions, you're less likely to be influenced by external circumstances or react impulsively. This gives you the composure that is a key component of gravitas.

2. **Master Your Body Language**

   o Your body speaks louder than words, and people subconsciously gauge your presence based on your physical demeanor. To cultivate gravitas, focus on maintaining a posture of **strength** and **composure**.

   o Stand tall, shoulders back, and move with purpose. Avoid fidgeting or unnecessary movements that can give off an impression of insecurity or indecision. A steady, grounded posture signals confidence and assurance.

3. **Speak Less, But Speak with Authority**

   o Gravitas is as much about what you don't say as it is about what you do. Those with gravitas understand the value of **silence** and **brevity**. They don't feel the need to fill every silence with words or to dominate conversations with long-winded speeches.

   o When you do speak, ensure that your words are **clear**, **intentional**, and **powerful**. Avoid empty words or superficial talk. Every statement should add value, whether it's sharing wisdom, offering a solution, or making a decisive declaration.

4. **Build Your Knowledge and Competence**

   o Gravitas is also rooted in **substance**—the depth of your knowledge and experience. The more competent you are in your field, the more naturally gravitas will flow from you.

   o Invest in continuous learning and personal growth. Read widely, seek mentorship, and constantly improve your skills. When you have a solid foundation of knowledge, you can speak with authority on a variety of subjects, which increases the respect others have for you.

5. **Stay True to Your Principles**

   o Gravitas is built upon **integrity**. People with gravitas don't change their principles to suit the situation or the crowd. They act according to their values, and they do so consistently.

   o Identify your core values and commit to living by them, no matter the circumstances. When others see that you are unshakable in your principles, they will begin to see you as someone worthy of respect and admiration.

◆ **Gravitas vs. Arrogance**

One of the most important distinctions to make when developing gravitas is the difference between **gravitas** and **arrogance**. While gravitas is built on substance, **arrogance** is often rooted in insecurity and a need to prove oneself. The key difference lies in **humility**.

- **Gravitas** doesn't need to boast or announce its presence—it simply **is**. It's calm, composed, and internally grounded.

- **Arrogance**, on the other hand, is often loud and flashy, attempting to prove superiority by putting others down. People with gravitas **lift others up**, whereas arrogant people often **look down** on others.

To avoid arrogance, focus on staying humble in your strength. Gravitas requires an **internal confidence** that doesn't need to constantly prove itself. Instead of trying to dominate, those with gravitas create an environment where **their presence** naturally influences and inspires respect.

◆ The Impact of Gravitas on Leadership

Gravitas is one of the most essential qualities of great leadership. A leader with gravitas commands respect without needing to exert control or dominate the conversation. People follow gravitas-driven leaders not because they fear them, but because they **trust** them to make the right decisions.

When you lead with gravitas:

- You inspire confidence in your team or followers, creating an environment where others can thrive.

- You create a sense of stability and clarity that allows those around you to focus on the mission at hand, knowing that they are in capable hands.

- You become the person others turn to for guidance, knowing that your decisions are made with wisdom, experience, and integrity.

Final Thoughts: The Silent Strength of Gravitas

Gravitas is the ultimate silent power. It's the deep, rooted strength that commands respect not through force, but through quiet authority. It's the presence that others instinctively feel—the feeling that you are someone who knows who they are, knows what they stand for, and is unwavering in their resolve.

Cultivating gravitas is a lifelong pursuit, but it is well worth the effort. As you continue to develop this essential quality, remember that gravitas is not something you seek externally. It is something that grows from within, through self-mastery, consistency, and an unwavering commitment to integrity. And when you embody this depth of character, respect and authority will follow naturally.

Building a Reputation of Depth

In a world that often values flash over substance, it is easy to be distracted by the allure of quick success, temporary validation, and superficial recognition. However, the most powerful and enduring form of respect comes from a reputation built on **depth**, **integrity**, and **consistency**—all hallmarks of true gravitas.

Building a reputation of depth doesn't happen overnight. It's a slow burn, a process that requires deliberate and thoughtful actions, an unwavering commitment to your values, and the patience to allow your actions to speak louder than words. This reputation is not about how many people know you or how loud you can shout about your achievements—it's about the **lasting impression** you leave on those who encounter you, and the quiet confidence you project in every situation.

A reputation of depth comes from being someone who:

- **Lives with authenticity**, never compromising on your core values.

- **Takes responsibility** for your actions, learning from mistakes and growing continuously.

- **Builds relationships based on trust and mutual respect** rather than convenience or status.

- **Leads by example**, demonstrating through your actions the kind of strength and wisdom that others admire.

In this section, we'll explore how you can begin to build a reputation that reflects your inner strength and self-mastery—one that endures and continues to inspire long after the fleeting trends of the moment have passed.

◆ **Start with Integrity**

The foundation of any lasting reputation is **integrity**. Your integrity is what people will remember about you long after they forget your achievements, your appearance, or your charisma. Integrity means staying true to your word, being honest even when it's uncomfortable, and ensuring that your actions align with your values.

To build a reputation of depth, you must:

- **Do what you say you'll do**: Be consistent in following through on your commitments. Whether it's a small promise or a major project, your word should be your bond.

- **Be transparent and honest**: People trust those who are upfront and honest. They may not always agree with you, but they will respect your commitment to the truth.

- **Stand by your principles**: Even when the pressure is high or the path isn't easy, stay committed to your values. When others see that you will not compromise on what matters most to you, they begin to trust you with their respect.

Building a reputation of integrity requires long-term vision—it's about doing what's right, not what's easy. And over time, this reputation will set you apart from others who are chasing the next trend or seeking immediate validation.

◆ **Be Consistent in Your Actions**

Gravitas doesn't come from a single moment of brilliance or a burst of charisma. It is the product of **consistent** and **intentional** actions that reflect your character. Every day you have an opportunity to reinforce your reputation, whether it's in the way you treat others, the decisions you make, or the way you handle challenges.

To build a reputation of depth through consistency:

- **Demonstrate reliability**: Be someone who others can count on, not just when it's convenient, but when it matters most. Whether it's keeping promises or maintaining a standard of excellence, your ability to consistently deliver builds trust.

- **Cultivate self-discipline**: Consistency requires discipline. When you develop habits that align with your highest goals, you send a clear signal that you are serious about your work, your relationships, and your commitments. This is where true gravitas grows.

- **Stay calm in the face of adversity**: In moments of crisis or challenge, it's easy to let emotions take over. But true depth is revealed when you maintain your composure and make thoughtful, measured decisions, even when others are losing their heads.

Gravitas is not about being perfect—it's about showing up every day, committed to improving, and acting in ways that align with your values.

◆ Prioritize Meaningful Relationships

One of the most effective ways to build a reputation of depth is by surrounding yourself with people who **value substance** over style. It's easy to gain superficial admiration, but true respect comes from those who recognize your character, your wisdom, and your inner strength.

To build relationships of depth:

- **Be present and genuinely interested**: Take the time to listen deeply when others speak. Ask questions that show you value their perspectives. When you invest in others, they'll invest in you.

- **Offer support without expectation**: Gravitas isn't about transactional relationships. It's about being there for others in a way that is selfless and authentic. Help others grow, and they will recognize your strength.

- **Develop emotional intelligence**: Understanding the emotions of others and knowing how to respond appropriately is a key part of building meaningful relationships. It's not about winning arguments or being right—it's about understanding others and offering thoughtful support.

When your relationships are built on trust, respect, and mutual growth, your reputation of depth will naturally expand. People will begin to see you as a person of influence, someone whose character and wisdom are invaluable.

◆ Lead with Humility and Service

A person with gravitas doesn't seek to be the center of attention. They lead with **humility** and **service**, putting the needs of others above their own desires for recognition. Humility doesn't mean minimizing your achievements or talents; it means using your strengths for the benefit of others without seeking constant validation.

To lead with humility and service:

- **Empower others**: A person with gravitas recognizes that leadership is not about being the loudest or most visible in the room—it's about **lifting others** up. Help people around you achieve their potential, and they will respect you for it.

- **Give credit where it's due**: Gravitas comes from being secure enough in your own worth that you don't need to take all the credit. Acknowledge the contributions of others and share successes. This builds trust and strengthens your reputation.

- **Lead by example**: Show up with a strong work ethic, integrity, and a commitment to excellence. When you set the standard, others will follow.

When you lead with humility and service, you not only build a reputation of depth—you build a legacy of influence that will last long after you've left the room.

◆ Be Patient with the Process

Building a reputation of depth takes time. It doesn't happen overnight, and it doesn't come from a single grand gesture. Instead, it's the result of **small,** consistent actions, year after year, that align with your principles and values.

In a world that often glorifies instant gratification, gravitas is a **long-term investment**. It requires you to **play the long game**—making decisions today that will continue to bear fruit for years to come.

To stay patient with the process:

- **Focus on the bigger picture**: Don't get caught up in immediate rewards or quick recognition. Stay focused on your long-term goals and your vision for your life. Let your actions align with that bigger vision.

- **Embrace the journey**: Recognize that the development of your character is a lifelong journey. Every challenge, every setback, and every success adds to the depth of your reputation.

- **Trust the process**: Trust that, over time, your actions will speak for themselves. Consistency, integrity, and wisdom will build a reputation that can't be easily shaken.

In the end, it's not about how fast you achieve your goals—it's about how you consistently show up, live with authenticity, and contribute to the world around you.

Final Thoughts: The Lasting Power of Depth

Building a reputation of depth is one of the most powerful ways to embody gravitas. It's about being a person who is known not for the flashiness of their actions, but for the weight of their character. When you cultivate this reputation, you will find that respect follows naturally—people will turn to you for guidance, they will trust your judgment, and they will recognize you as someone whose presence brings value.

Remember, gravitas is not about creating an image for others to admire. It's about being so rooted in your own values, actions, and integrity that your reputation grows from the inside out, becoming a lasting testament to the power of **substance over style**.

Slowing Down Your Thinking and Speaking

In a fast-paced world, where everything is moving at the speed of light, there is an immense power in **slowing down**—in both your thinking and your speaking. This isn't about being less productive or taking longer to get things done. It's about **deliberateness** and **clarity**—cultivating the ability to **pause**, to reflect, and to respond with purpose rather than react out of haste or impulse.

People with gravitas understand that **thoughtful action** always trumps **hasty reaction**. They possess the self-control to resist the urge to rush into decisions or speak without considering their words. They know that the most powerful responses are often the most measured and intentional.

Slowing down your thinking and speaking is a critical component of developing gravitas. It helps you avoid the trap of **reacting emotionally**, makes you appear more **thoughtful and composed**, and ensures that your words carry **weight**. A person who speaks slowly and thoughtfully creates an impression of **depth**—of someone who has carefully considered every word, not someone who is merely trying to fill the silence.

In this section, we'll explore why slowing down can increase your influence, how to consciously slow down your thinking and speaking, and the impact it can have on your gravitas.

◆ The Power of Deliberate Thinking

In a world where speed is often celebrated, deliberate thinking can be your greatest asset. When you slow down your thoughts, you create space for deeper reflection, clearer understanding, and more effective decision-making. Quick decisions and spontaneous reactions often lead to **mistakes**, misunderstandings, or **miscommunications**. But when you allow yourself to pause, even momentarily, you give yourself the opportunity to respond in a way that reflects **wisdom** rather than impulse.

Here's why deliberate thinking matters:

- **Clarity of thought**: When you slow down your thinking, you allow yourself to fully process the situation. You can take in all the relevant information, consider the potential outcomes, and make a decision based on logic, not emotion.

- **Avoids rash decisions**: When we rush our thinking, we often make decisions based on immediate emotions, biases, or external pressures. Slowing down helps you **filter out distractions**, allowing you to think with a clear mind and make decisions rooted in logic and integrity.

- **Shows composure**: When you take the time to think things through, people notice your **calmness** and **composure**. They see that you aren't rushed or overwhelmed, which naturally increases your gravitas.

To slow down your thinking:

- **Pause before reacting**: In any situation, give yourself a moment to breathe and consider your response. This momentary pause allows you to assess the situation and respond thoughtfully.

- **Practice mindfulness**: Mindfulness techniques can help center your mind and focus your thoughts. Take time to practice being present, whether through meditation or simple breathing exercises.

- **Ask clarifying questions**: If you find yourself unsure or overwhelmed by a situation, ask questions to gather more information before making decisions. This slows down your reaction time and ensures that you understand the full scope of what's happening.

Slowing down your thinking leads to more effective problem-solving, clearer decision-making, and a stronger sense of **control**—three pillars that contribute to your gravitas.

◆ The Impact of Slower Speech

Your speech, just like your thoughts, carries an immense amount of power. When you slow down the pace at which you speak, your words hold more

weight. You are no longer simply filling space with sound; you are **delivering messages** that carry meaning, resonance, and authority.

In a world where people are often talking over one another, speaking quickly, and trying to keep up with the pace of conversation, **slowing down** can be a game-changer. It gives your words the **space to land**, allowing your listeners to fully absorb and reflect on what you've said. When you speak slowly, your words become more **thoughtful**, **intentional**, and impactful.

Here's why slowing down your speech is essential:

- **Conveys confidence**: Speaking slowly and deliberately signals that you are not afraid of silence. You are confident enough to give yourself time to think and to speak in a way that feels **measured** and **composed**.

- **Improves clarity**: When you speak too quickly, your message often gets lost in translation. People may miss key points or misunderstand your intentions. Slower speech ensures that your message is clear, concise, and understood.

- **Captures attention**: People naturally listen more intently when someone speaks with a measured pace. Your slow and deliberate speech creates **tension** and draws in your audience, making them eager to hear what you say next.

- **Avoids unnecessary words**: When we speak too quickly, we tend to use filler words like "um," "like," and "you know," which can detract from the impact of our message. Slowing down allows you to focus on the quality of your words, rather than the quantity.

To slow down your speech:

- **Pause regularly**: Take intentional pauses in between sentences or thoughts. This not only gives you time to think but also lets your words settle with your listeners.

- **Breathe between phrases**: Use your breath to guide the pacing of your speech. Pausing to breathe allows your body to relax, which in turn slows the rate at which you speak.

- **Enunciate clearly**: Speaking slowly allows you to articulate your words more clearly, making it easier for others to understand and absorb what you're saying.

- **Be comfortable with silence**: Silence doesn't have to be awkward. Embrace moments of quiet between your thoughts. This will enhance the impact of your speech and show your ability to **command attention** without force.

◆ The Effect on Your Gravitas

Slowing down your thinking and speaking directly enhances your gravitas. When you take the time to process your thoughts and speak with intent, you exude a calm confidence that others find magnetic. This **slowness** does not indicate hesitation or weakness—it signals that you are **in control** of yourself and your environment. You have the power to decide when to speak, what to say, and how to deliver your message.

The impact of slowing down on your gravitas is profound:

- **Enhances your authority**: People naturally gravitate toward those who speak and act with purpose. When you slow down, you signal to others that you have the **time and presence** to consider their perspective and speak with authority.

- **Increases your impact**: Because your words carry weight, people are more likely to take your advice seriously and follow your lead. Your thoughts and actions are measured and strategic, which inspires trust and respect.

- **Exudes calm strength**: A man with gravitas is never rushed. He doesn't feel the need to hurry through life's decisions or moments. By slowing down your responses, you project an aura of inner strength that naturally draws people to you.

◆ **Practical Tips for Slowing Down**

- **Take a deep breath** before responding in conversations or making decisions. This moment of pause can ground you and help slow down your thought process.

- **Practice mindfulness** daily. Engage in simple breathing exercises or meditation to enhance your ability to remain present in every moment.

- **Delay your responses** in conversations. Instead of answering immediately, give yourself a moment to collect your thoughts. This helps you avoid speaking impulsively and ensures that you respond with clarity.

- **Rehearse intentional speaking**: In practice, focus on speaking with purpose. Even if you're just talking to a friend or family member, work on speaking slowly and deliberately, avoiding rushed words and ensuring each sentence has meaning.

Final Thoughts: The Art of Slowing Down

Slowing down is not about **doing less**—it's about doing things with **greater intention**. In a world that's often defined by urgency, those who take their time to think, speak, and act are the ones who command true influence and respect. By slowing down your thinking and speech, you allow your actions to reflect your gravitas, ensuring that your presence leaves a deep, lasting impression on everyone you encounter.

When you learn to slow down, you become more than just a participant in life's conversations—you become the one who **guides** them, with composure, authority, and depth.

Aligning Your Actions with Your Values

At the core of masculine gravitas is an unshakable alignment between your actions and your values. This alignment is what separates those who merely talk about strength, character, and integrity from those who truly embody it. A man of gravitas lives in accordance with his principles, consistently demonstrating through his actions what he believes to be important. He doesn't simply speak about his values—he **embodies** them in every aspect of his life.

When your actions align with your values, you become a **walking embodiment** of authenticity. Your presence becomes more powerful because it's built on something rock-solid: a deep and unshakable understanding of who you are and what you stand for. People sense this alignment, and it becomes a beacon that draws them in, builds trust, and commands respect.

In this section, we'll explore why aligning your actions with your values is essential for cultivating gravitas, how to identify your core values, and practical steps to ensure your behavior consistently reflects these values.

◆ Why Alignment Matters

In a world where people often project one image but live by another, the power of alignment cannot be overstated. Misalignment between words and actions is a glaring contradiction that undermines trust and erodes the credibility of anyone who displays it.

When you align your actions with your values, it creates:

- **Consistency**: People know what to expect from you. They see that your behavior is predictable and rooted in a firm foundation of integrity.

- **Authenticity**: You stop feeling the need to "prove" yourself because you simply are who you are. When you act in accordance with your beliefs, you no longer have to fake anything. What you see is what you get.

- **Trust**: Others are more likely to respect and follow you when your actions are consistent with your values. When you walk the talk, you gain credibility and influence—qualities that are essential for gravitas.

- **Inner Peace**: When your actions reflect your values, you live in harmony with yourself. This inner alignment breeds confidence and a deep sense of personal strength that others can feel.

◆ Identifying Your Core Values

Before you can align your actions with your values, you need to first **define** what your values actually are. This is a deeply personal process that requires introspection and clarity. Your values are the guiding principles by which you live, and they shape every decision you make—from how you treat others to how you navigate life's challenges.

Here's how you can begin identifying your core values:

- **Reflect on your past experiences**: Think back to moments when you felt the most fulfilled, proud, or at peace with yourself. What were you doing? Who were you with? What were the underlying principles that guided your actions in those moments?

- **Identify your role models**: Who do you admire, and why? What qualities do they possess that resonate with you? Often, the traits you admire in others point to values you hold dear.

- **Consider your non-negotiables**: What can you not compromise on? These are the principles that, if violated, would cause you to feel disoriented or out of integrity.

- **List the values that matter most to you**: Write down a list of values that resonate with you (e.g., honesty, loyalty, courage, compassion, discipline). Rank them from most important to least important. This will give you a clear picture of where to focus your energy.

Once you've identified your values, the next step is to integrate them into your everyday life. If you find your values are inconsistent or unclear, take the time to revisit them until you have a crystal-clear understanding of what you stand for.

◆ Aligning Your Daily Actions with Your Values

Aligning your actions with your values doesn't require perfection—it requires consistency. Your values should be reflected in both **big decisions** and **small interactions**. It's the daily, seemingly insignificant moments where the truth of your character shows through. Your behavior must be a mirror image of your beliefs, from how you treat others to how you approach challenges.

To align your actions with your values, consider the following strategies:

- **Make conscious choices**: Every day, you're presented with decisions, both large and small. Ask yourself: "Does this decision align with my core values?" When your actions are rooted in your values, even small decisions have an impact on your overall sense of integrity.

- **Respond, don't react**: Life presents you with unexpected situations. In these moments, it's easy to react impulsively, but your values should act as a guiding compass for how you respond. Pause before you act—ask yourself what your values demand of you in that moment, and choose the response that reflects them.

- **Model your values for others**: A man of gravitas doesn't just talk about his values—he shows others what they look like in action. By being a living example of your principles, you naturally inspire those around you to embody similar traits.

- **Consistency over time**: Alignment isn't something you achieve once and forget. It's an ongoing process. Revisit your values regularly, check in with your actions, and ensure you're living in alignment. The more consistently you embody your values, the more they become an inherent part of who you are.

◆ The Impact of Living in Alignment

When you consistently align your actions with your values, the effects on your gravitas are profound. Here's how this alignment impacts your life and the way others perceive you:

- **Increased influence**: People are drawn to those who act with integrity and consistency. When you align your actions with your values, you automatically gain influence because others know they can trust you to act in accordance with your beliefs.

- **Stronger relationships**: Your relationships deepen when people know they can rely on you to act in line with your values. They see you as dependable, authentic, and someone they can count on in difficult times.

- **Inner strength**: There's a certain quiet strength that comes from knowing you are living according to your true self. You feel secure in your decisions and confident in your interactions, which naturally amplifies your gravitas.

- **Long-term respect**: Values-driven behavior may not always win immediate praise or recognition, but over time, it earns you the respect of those who recognize the **depth** of your character. This respect is lasting and solidifies your reputation as someone whose presence commands authority and influence.

◆ Maintaining Alignment Amid Challenges

Living in alignment with your values can be challenging, especially when external pressures tempt you to compromise or act against your core beliefs. But a man with gravitas rises to the occasion, even when it's difficult. The ability to maintain your values, even in challenging circumstances, is what truly **cements your reputation** as someone of depth and integrity.

Here are a few ways to maintain alignment during tough times:

- **Pause before making big decisions**: In moments of high stress or pressure, take a step back. Reflect on your values before deciding how to proceed. This pause gives you the space to make choices that are in alignment with your true self.

- **Practice self-awareness**: Regularly check in with yourself. Are you acting in accordance with your values? If not, identify where the disconnect is happening and course-correct.

- **Seek guidance when needed**: If you're facing a particularly challenging situation, don't hesitate to seek counsel from others who embody the values you respect. They can help provide clarity and support as you navigate tough decisions.

Final Thoughts: The Power of Aligned Living

When your actions align with your values, you no longer have to worry about maintaining a facade. The strength of your character speaks for itself, and your reputation grows as a result. Living in alignment isn't about avoiding mistakes— it's about **owning your actions** and consistently choosing to act in accordance with your deepest beliefs.

This alignment becomes the foundation upon which your gravitas is built. It creates an unshakable sense of inner peace and external confidence that others can't help but respect. Over time, your commitment to living authentically will cement your place as a person whose presence commands attention and admiration.

8

Personal Power – Opening Your Space

The Difference Between Power and Force

In the realm of masculine frame, understanding the distinction between **power** and **force** is crucial. While they may seem similar at first glance, they are fundamentally different energies—and mastering both is key to cultivating true personal power.

Force is loud, aggressive, and often rooted in fear or insecurity. It demands attention, but it lacks the depth and substance that sustain long-term respect and influence. It is a **push** rather than a pull, and it often feels like a battle to be fought. Force comes from a place of needing to control, dominate, or assert oneself, frequently at the expense of others' autonomy or peace.

Power, on the other hand, is quiet, calm, and rooted in confidence and authenticity. It is the ability to influence, guide, and shape the world around you without needing to force anything. Power comes from within; it doesn't need to be loud to be heard. It is the strength to **create** space, to command attention, and to inspire others—without effort, without aggression, and without fear.

In this section, we will explore the key differences between power and force, why power is the more sustainable and effective form of influence, and how you can tap into your personal power to influence your surroundings without force.

◆ Force: The Illusion of Control

When you rely on **force**, you often end up **pushing** or **forcing** situations to unfold according to your desires. Whether it's an attempt to dominate a conversation, control a situation, or impose your will on others, force comes from a place of **urgency** and **fear**. It's driven by an underlying belief that you must dominate your surroundings to be effective.

But force has limitations:

- **Short-term gains**: Force may give you the immediate appearance of control, but it doesn't lead to lasting influence. People might comply in the moment, but their respect for you doesn't deepen, and they may resist in the long run.

- **Creates resistance**: People generally don't respond well to force. Whether through verbal aggression, coercion, or manipulation, force often breeds resentment or withdrawal. It's the metaphorical equivalent of pushing against a closed door—the more you push, the more resistance you face.

- **Unsustainable**: Force requires constant exertion. You must continually push, dominate, and demand. This can be exhausting, emotionally draining, and ultimately unsustainable. When you rely on force, you're always **chasing after control**, and that takes a toll on your mental and physical energy.

Force comes from the need to **prove** yourself—often as a way of compensating for a lack of inner confidence. People who rely on force often act from a place of **insecurity** or **lack**. This is why, despite the immediate success it may bring, force never creates the **genuine influence** or **lasting respect** that power does.

◆ **Power: The Art of Presence and Influence**

In contrast, **power** is subtle, measured, and emanates from a place of inner strength. When you possess true personal power, you don't need to force anything; things **happen naturally** around you because you have the ability to influence, guide, and inspire with your presence alone. Power is not about imposing your will on others—it's about **creating space** for others to see your confidence and choose to follow your lead.

Here's why power is more effective and sustainable than force:

- **Rooted in confidence, not fear**: True power is grounded in self-assurance. You don't need to prove anything to anyone. You are secure in who you are, and this quiet confidence speaks volumes. You become a magnet for respect and admiration without needing to assert yourself aggressively.

- **Influence without domination**: Rather than forcing your agenda onto others, you **invite** them into your space. Power is about influence through inspiration, persuasion, and leadership. People follow because they believe in you, not because you're making them.

- **Creates flow**: Power has the ability to create harmony. When you exude power, others naturally gravitate toward you. You don't have to fight for attention, approval, or validation. Instead, you open the space for others to see and respond to your presence. Power allows for **smooth transitions**, **effective leadership**, and **long-lasting influence**.

- **Sustainable**: Power doesn't require constant effort or energy. It is an **enduring quality** that grows with time. The more you cultivate your inner power, the less you need to exert external force to get results.

Power is about **leading with intent** and **creating opportunity** without forcing your way. It's the quiet strength that attracts others and draws them into your sphere of influence naturally.

◆ How Power Transforms Your Presence

The beauty of power is that it doesn't need to shout to be heard. In fact, the more you rely on power, the more it amplifies your **presence**. This presence is felt by those around you without any overt action on your part. It's your **energy**, your **vibration**, and your **confidence** that create the space for others to be drawn to you.

Here's how power transforms your presence:

- **Magnetic energy**: When you move through the world with power, you create a pull—a quiet gravitational force that draws others to you. People can sense your confidence, stability, and strength, and they are naturally inclined to follow your lead.

- **Commanding respect**: Unlike force, which demands respect through aggression, power earns it through authenticity. You don't need to impose anything; your actions and demeanor demand recognition. You command respect by being the embodiment of the qualities you represent.

- **Presence in silence**: Power doesn't rely on words or constant action. Sometimes, your **stillness**—your ability to remain centered and calm in the face of chaos—speaks louder than any words ever could. Power is found in the quiet moments, where your presence alone shifts the energy of a room.

When you stop relying on force and start cultivating power, your entire way of being changes. You become **someone whose presence** is felt long before you speak or act. You are the center of influence because you don't need to control the situation—**you guide it** with calm confidence.

◆ Cultivating Personal Power

Developing true power involves cultivating a mindset and presence that emanates from the inside out. Unlike force, which requires constant exertion, power comes from a place of **self-awareness**, **inner strength**, and **authenticity**. It's about trusting yourself to create space for your influence without needing to dominate others.

Here's how to cultivate personal power:

- **Build inner confidence**: The foundation of personal power is confidence. Take the time to develop your self-assurance through knowledge, self-reflection, and experiences that challenge you. The more you believe in your own worth and capabilities, the more powerful you become.

- **Develop emotional control**: Power comes from a place of emotional stability. Learn to master your emotions so that you don't react impulsively or from a place of insecurity. Practice mindfulness, meditation, and deep breathing to center yourself.

- **Exude authenticity**: Be true to yourself. When your actions, words, and thoughts are aligned with your authentic self, you exude an undeniable confidence that commands respect.

- **Lead through example**: Power is not about telling others what to do— it's about showing them through your actions. Be a role model of the qualities you wish to inspire in others.

Final Thoughts: Power Over Force

Understanding the difference between power and force is a transformative realization in the journey toward masculine frame. While force may yield short-term victories, power is the key to enduring influence, respect, and leadership. Power is about creating space, leading through example, and inspiring others without imposing your will upon them.

When you embrace the quiet strength of personal power, you free yourself from the need to dominate, control, or force your way through life. Instead, you become a force in and of yourself, shaping the world around you with calm confidence and unwavering authenticity.

Internal vs. External Power

To understand true masculine power, you must distinguish between its two primary forms: **internal power** and **external power**. The difference between the two is not just about source—it's about **sustainability**, **authenticity**, and **influence**.

External power is visible. It's status, money, physical strength, rank, titles, and social dominance. It's the kind of power the world often celebrates—loud, tangible, and easy to recognize.

Internal power, on the other hand, is invisible. It's composure under pressure. It's emotional self-mastery. It's self-respect, purpose, alignment, and a calm that cannot be shaken by circumstance. It doesn't shout, it doesn't boast, and yet, it moves mountains.

Masculine frame begins with internal power. Without it, external power is hollow—an unstable house built on sand. But when internal power is strong, even without wealth, status, or titles, your presence is undeniable.

◆ External Power: The Surface Advantage

External power can be a useful tool. In the modern world, people often respond to it because it's easily recognized:

- A man with a high-ranking title or visible wealth is often given attention.

- Physical dominance can create an illusion of control.

- Social status can attract temporary respect.

But here's the key: **external power is conditional**. It can be taken away. A job title can be lost. Money can disappear. Looks can fade. If your sense of self-worth is built solely on these things, you're always at risk. And worse, people will eventually sense the **fragility** behind the front.

External power without internal grounding leads to insecurity masked as dominance. That's when men become performative—aggressive, arrogant, reactive—because they fear being exposed. They push harder, talk louder, and try to control more, not realizing their energy is fueled by **lack**, not strength.

There is nothing wrong with building external power—**but it must be built on the foundation of internal power**, not used as a substitute for it.

◆ Internal Power: The Unshakable Core

Internal power is the root of a man's masculine frame. It's silent, but its presence is commanding. It's the reason some men can walk into a room, say nothing, and shift the energy. They don't have to force respect—it follows them.

Internal power is built through:

- **Emotional regulation**: You are not ruled by impulse or reactivity. You respond with clarity, not chaos.

- **Self-trust**: You've proven to yourself—through challenge, discomfort, and discipline—that you can be relied upon. That's where true confidence is born.

- **Purpose and alignment**: You live according to your values. Your decisions are not dictated by fear or people-pleasing but by what you know is right.

- **Grounded presence**: You're comfortable in silence. You don't seek validation. You carry yourself with calm certainty.

- **Resilience**: You can lose everything external and still remain centered. That's real power.

When internal power is present, everything external becomes an extension—not a crutch. Your frame doesn't collapse when tested. You don't become reactive when challenged. You don't shrink when others shine.

◆ The Hierarchy: Internal First, External Second

Many men pursue external power first, hoping it will fix internal insecurity. It doesn't. In fact, it often makes it worse. They build empires on unstable ground—living in fear of being found out, of losing what they've gained, of facing their own emptiness once the noise dies down.

But when you build **internal power first**, everything changes:

- External power becomes easier to attract because you're not chasing it from need—you're pulling it from abundance.

- Respect lasts longer because people trust your **substance**, not just your image.

- Influence deepens because you're not just performing strength—you are strength.

You become a man who does not flinch under pressure, who does not need the room to validate him, and who does not crumble when stripped of titles or tools. That's power. **That's frame.**

◆ Embodying Both Without Losing Yourself

The most powerful men in the world are those who have **both** internal and external power—and know the difference.

They use their wealth, status, or platform as tools, not identities. They are not owned by what they've built—they are still the same man when it's all gone. That's because their **sense of self was forged in silence, discipline, and solitude**, not applause.

If you want to be unshakable, focus on the invisible before the visible. Develop the muscles that can't be seen: discipline, integrity, emotional stillness, patience, purpose. The rest will follow—and when it does, it will **serve you**, not define you.

Final Thoughts: The Power That Cannot Be Taken

External power can open doors. Internal power determines whether you can walk through them with presence, with influence, and with dignity.

A man who has developed internal power is not addicted to attention, approval, or dominance. He is free from needing to perform. That is the kind of power no one can take away. That is the kind of power that shapes legacies.

Build your world from the inside out.

Energy Control: Presence Over Pressure

There is a difference between being **intense** and being **impactful**. Many men, in their pursuit of power, overexert. They show up loud, fast, and eager to prove something. They lean in too far, speak too much, try too hard. The result? Pressure—not presence.

True presence doesn't come from pressure. It comes from controlled energy.

A man with presence doesn't need to be the loudest, smartest, or most dominant person in the room. He knows that energy, when **centered and regulated**, creates gravity. He draws people in without chasing them. He influences situations without overpowering them.

Your control over your **energetic output**—your tone, pace, body language, and emotional intensity—is a cornerstone of masculine frame. When you master this control, you shift from creating **pressure** to embodying **presence**. You stop trying to force outcomes, and instead, your very being begins to shape them.

◆ **Pressure: The Overcompensation of Uncentered Energy**

Pressure is what you create when you don't trust your own presence to be enough.

It shows up as:

- Talking too much, too fast, or too loud

- Constantly explaining yourself or trying to convince others

- Interrupting or rushing interactions

- Fidgeting, pacing, or leaking nervous energy

- Needing to be right or be seen

Pressure makes people back away—not out of fear, but because it signals **neediness**, insecurity, or inner chaos. Even if you say the right words, pressure makes people feel like they're being pulled, not drawn.

And that pull creates tension. It repels. Because **masculine energy, at its highest, is not forceful—it's grounded**.

◆ Presence: The Quiet Power of Centered Energy

Presence is what you embody when your energy is contained, not scattered. It is the opposite of pressure. It feels calm, still, and magnetic. People can feel it the moment you walk into a room—not because you demand attention, but because you **don't need it**.

Presence communicates:

- **I am here, and I am enough.**

- **I do not chase. I attract.**

- **I trust myself to handle what comes.**

It's an energetic stillness that says: "I've done the inner work. I'm not performing—I'm rooted." That rootedness makes others want to follow you, listen to you, and align with you—without you ever having to push.

Presence doesn't require intensity. It requires **self-mastery**. That's why it's so rare—and why it's so powerful.

◆ Developing Energetic Control

You don't need to withdraw or be passive to avoid pressure. You need to learn how to **hold your energy**, like a coiled spring—ready but contained. This is what creates tension in the best sense: a magnetic field around you that others feel, even in silence.

To control your energy:

1. **Ground yourself before you speak or enter a space**

   Take a breath. Feel your feet on the ground. Slow your heart rate. Enter with awareness, not urgency. Remind yourself: "I bring the calm. I don't chase the room—I shape it."

2. **Speak slower, with more space between your words**

This signals confidence and allows your message to land. Fast talkers often feel like they're rushing past their own uncertainty. Slowness equals control.

3. **Limit unnecessary movements**

Fidgeting, shifting, over-gesturing—all signal uncontained energy. Hold still. Make each movement intentional. Stillness is presence in physical form.

4. **Let silence do some of the talking**

Don't rush to fill space. The man who is comfortable with silence radiates calm dominance. Use pauses to let others feel your weight before you speak again.

5. **Regulate your emotional intensity**

You don't have to smile nervously or over-emote to be liked. You don't have to overreact to prove you care. Show up steady. People trust the man who can **feel deeply** without being **swept away** by the feeling.

◆ **The Masculine Field: Creating Impact Without Volume**

When your energy is controlled, your presence becomes a **field**—something others feel when they come near you. It softens aggression, calms chaos, and gives others permission to relax and respect. You lead not through volume, but through vibration.

This is the difference between someone who takes up space and someone who fills it. One demands room. The other **creates** it. That's the essence of energy control. **Not to dominate—but to stabilize.** Not to pressure—but to project calm certainty.

And that's what makes you powerful—not your words, not your status, but the **way your energy speaks** before you ever open your mouth.

Final Thoughts: Control the Energy, Own the Room

In every room, there are those who demand attention—and those who **earn it** through silent gravity. Be the latter.

Learn to hold your energy like a blade—sharp, steady, and never wasted. When you choose presence over pressure, you stop chasing impact and start **embodying** it. You become the calm anchor others seek in chaos.

This is the power of energy control. This is the quiet fire of a man in full command of himself.

Power Rituals and Habits

Power doesn't arrive suddenly. It's cultivated. Not in the heat of battle or the chaos of conflict, but in the quiet, repetitive moments when no one is watching. A man's power is forged in his rituals—daily, intentional practices that align his mind, body, and energy.

The difference between a man who moves through life reactively and one who commands a room without saying a word is often this: the latter has habits that support his frame. He trains it. Conditions it. Lives it.

These rituals aren't about being rigid or robotic—they're about tapping into your personal rhythm, sharpening your focus, and strengthening the internal authority that others feel before you speak.

Let's break down how you can establish the daily systems that keep your energy centered, your presence sharp, and your masculine frame unshakable.

◆ The Purpose of Rituals: Anchoring Your Power

Power rituals are anchors. They center you in your purpose and prevent the world from pulling you off course. These routines are less about performance and more about presence—about building structure that reinforces your internal power every single day.

136

Here's why they matter:

- They protect your energy from external noise and distraction.

- They reaffirm your identity, reminding you of who you are and what you're building.

- They create momentum—power doesn't come from one heroic act, but from thousands of small, consistent ones.

- They reduce mental clutter and emotional drift. When your days are built on purpose-driven repetition, clarity and discipline become automatic.

Your rituals don't need to be complicated. They need to be intentional.

◆ Morning Rituals: Starting From Center

How you begin the day determines the energy you carry into it. Power is not about rushing out the door—it's about taking ownership of the day before the world makes demands of you.

A high-frame morning ritual might include:

1. Waking in silence: No phone. No stimulation. Just presence. Start with five minutes of stillness or meditation. Anchor yourself before the noise begins.

2. Movement: Train your body to respond to challenge first thing. A workout, stretching, or cold exposure reminds your nervous system: *I am capable, I am resilient, I am ready.*

3. Journaling or intention-setting: One line is enough. Ask yourself: *What kind of man do I want to be today?* Then live into that.

4. Discipline before dopamine: Delay digital distractions. Don't give away your attention the moment you wake. Let the first part of your day serve your vision, not someone else's.

This is how you start with power: not by reacting, but by owning the moment.

◆ Midday Habits: Recalibration and Control

As the day unfolds, distractions multiply. That's why powerful men recalibrate. You don't just hope to stay composed—you engineer your composure.

Power-maintaining habits for the day:

- Scheduled solitude: Even 5–10 minutes of silence in the middle of the day can restore clarity. No stimulation, no conversation. Just stillness. This resets your nervous system.

- Posture check-ins: Your physical frame affects your mental state. Shoulders back, jaw relaxed, slow breath. You realign your presence through your posture.

- Energy audit: Ask yourself: *Where am I leaking energy?* Identify the conversations, thoughts, or habits draining your strength—and close the leaks.

- Tension release: Power is not tightness. It's relaxed readiness. Throughout the day, scan your body for tension—jaw, neck, shoulders—and release it.

Midday rituals keep your internal engine calibrated. Even under pressure, they help you remain calm, not reactive.

◆ Evening Rituals: Reflection and Closure

The way you close your day determines whether you carry it into tomorrow—or let it serve your evolution.

An evening ritual strengthens your masculine frame through:

- Decompression: Step out of performance mode. This might be a walk, music, reading—something that helps your system transition from "doing" to "being."

- Reflection: Ask: *Where was I powerful today? Where did I leak?* Write one insight. Learn from yourself.

- Gratitude and grounding: End your day in appreciation, not anxiety. Power expands when you acknowledge what's working—not just what needs fixing.

- Sleep discipline: True power requires restoration. Set a wind-down routine and stick to it. Guard your sleep like your life depends on it—because your clarity, confidence, and composure do.

Evenings are not for escape. They're for integration. That's how you rise stronger the next day.

- Weekly or Monthly Power Practices

Beyond daily rituals, a powerful man steps back regularly to reorient his trajectory. A few ideas:

- Digital detox days: Unplug completely. Reclaim your attention and mental stillness.

- Solo reflection time: Take 1–2 hours alone—no distractions, no agenda. Let your deeper self speak.

- Nature immersion: Reconnect with your primal self. No signal. Just silence, earth, breath, and presence.

- Quarterly check-ins: Review your progress. Ask: *Am I becoming the man I've committed to? Where am I drifting?*

These higher-level rituals renew your vision and remind you: you are the architect of your reality.

Final Thoughts: Ritual Is Power Made Visible

Anyone can be disciplined for a moment. But a man of power builds his frame through rhythm. His habits aren't just boxes to check—they're the architecture of his presence. They are how he remains calm in chaos, grounded in temptation, and unshakable in uncertainty.

Power doesn't just live in what you do publicly. It's rooted in what you rehearse privately.

Choose your rituals. Keep them sacred.

Because how you live—when no one's watching—is exactly what they'll feel, when everyone is.

9

Shaping Reality - Influence

Psychological Levels of Influence

Influence is not about manipulation, persuasion tricks, or clever phrasing. True influence is about shaping the **reality** of others through your **energy, clarity, and consistency**. The most powerful men influence not just decisions—they influence **identity**, **beliefs**, and **emotional states**.

To wield influence consciously and ethically, you must understand the **levels** at which influence operates. The deeper you go, the more lasting—and less visible—your impact becomes. Influence begins at the surface but deepens through presence, alignment, and psychological mastery.

Let's explore the five key psychological levels of influence and how you can embody them as a man with a calm heart and a steel spine.

♦ **Level 1: Environmental Influence – Controlling the Frame**

The most surface-level form of influence is through **context**: the space, energy, and environment you create. People subconsciously adapt their behavior based on the room they're in, the tone set, and the **frame you hold**.

Examples:

- The man who walks in calm and unshaken sets the emotional tone of the room.

- A leader who speaks with composure can bring an agitated group into alignment without raising his voice.

- Simply how you sit, breathe, or pause can shift the energy around you.

You don't need to speak to influence at this level—**you simply show up with presence**. Control the environment, and you start to shape behavior.

◆ *Practice:* When entering a room, ask yourself: *What energy am I introducing? What emotional state am I leading others into by my presence alone?*

◆ **Level 2: Behavioral Influence – Leading Through Action**

People are influenced by **what you do**, far more than by what you say. When your behavior is consistent, grounded, and calm under pressure, people notice— even if they never mention it. Influence at this level is about **modeling**, not commanding.

You shape others by:

- Demonstrating restraint in conflict

- Showing discipline in your routines

- Holding standards in your words, time, and actions

- Following through even when it's uncomfortable

People begin to **mirror** what you embody. They trust you, not because you've sold them something—but because you live it.

◆ *Practice:* Let your actions do the talking. Before trying to persuade, ask: *Am I living in a way that makes my words credible?*

◆ **Level 3: Emotional Influence – Regulating the Nervous System**

This level is often overlooked, yet it's one of the most powerful: the ability to influence **how others feel** around you. Most people are emotionally reactive, easily thrown off course by tone, tension, or challenge. A man with internal power regulates his own nervous system—and by doing so, **stabilizes others**.

- When you remain calm while someone escalates, they begin to calm down.

- When you listen fully without rushing to respond, they feel seen and safe.

- When you speak slowly, breathe deeply, and remain relaxed, others subconsciously attune to that energy.

This is not manipulation. It's **emotional leadership**. You're not fixing people—you're simply becoming the strongest energetic anchor in the room. And people naturally align with the most grounded energy in their space.

◆ *Practice:* In any interaction, ask: *What emotion am I helping this person access? Am I radiating calm, clarity, and security—or am I leaking reactivity?*

◆ **Level 4: Cognitive Influence – Shaping Beliefs and Perception**

Now we move deeper: influencing how people **think**.

At this level, your influence shapes:

- The questions people ask themselves

- The beliefs they hold about what's possible

- The mental models they use to make decisions

You do this not by lecturing or convincing, but by:

- Asking powerful questions that challenge assumptions

- Speaking with clarity and conviction

- Offering new frames that rewire old thinking

- Living in such alignment that your perspective becomes persuasive by default

Example: Instead of saying "You need to be more disciplined," you ask, "What would change for you if you trusted yourself to follow through?"

Cognitive influence is subtle, but deep. It makes people rethink reality—and thank you for it later.

◆ *Practice:* Trade advice for questions. Seek to open minds, not win debates.

◆ **Level 5: Identity Influence – Shaping Who They Believe They Are**

This is the most profound and long-lasting level of influence: helping someone transform their **self-image**.

If you influence a person's environment, their behavior may shift. If you shape their beliefs, their thinking evolves. But if you help someone see themselves differently, **everything changes**—permanently.

This level requires:

- Deep trust

- Consistent modeling of higher standards

- The ability to see and speak to someone's **potential**, not just their patterns

When a man tells another, "You don't need to prove anything—you already have it in you," and he says it with conviction, groundedness, and lived example, it can **rewire years of self-doubt** in seconds. The man who influences identity becomes a catalyst for transformation—not because he controls, but because he believes.

◆ *Practice:* Lead others to a higher version of themselves by being that version first. Speak to who they can become—not just who they've been.

Final Thoughts: Influence That Echoes

The strongest influence is not always the most obvious. It doesn't come from dominance, cleverness, or pressure—it comes from **alignment**.

The man who lives in congruence—mind, body, and action—is the man others **want to follow**. Because he's not just talking. He's not just pushing. He's **being** the message. To shape reality, begin with your own. The world will follow the man who walks his truth—calmly, relentlessly, and without compromise.

Emotional Regulation in Social Dynamics

In every room you enter, there are two forces at play: the **emotions people bring in**, and the **emotions people absorb**. If you cannot regulate your own emotional state, someone else will do it for you. Either you lead the energy—or you get pulled into the current.

In masculine frame, **emotional regulation is non-negotiable**. It's not about being emotionless. It's about being emotionally sovereign. You don't suppress emotions—you own them, hold them, and direct them. This is what separates grounded presence from reactive energy.

When you're in command of your emotional state, you become the anchor in a storm. People look to you—not because you're the loudest, but because you're the most centered.

◆ Why Emotional Regulation Is Influence

Social dynamics are emotional exchanges long before they're intellectual ones. People don't just hear what you say—they **feel who you are**.

You influence most when you can:

- Stay calm when others are anxious

- Stay respectful when others are defensive

- Stay neutral when others are trying to provoke

The moment you react emotionally—especially with anger, defensiveness, or neediness—you surrender your frame. And when you lose your frame, you lose influence.

A regulated man remains unshaken. His energy doesn't spike, even in heated interactions. He listens without rushing to speak. He decides instead of reacts. This makes him rare—and magnetic.

◆ Social Triggers That Break Frame

To stay regulated, you must first recognize what **triggers** you.

Common social triggers that knock men out of frame:

- Being interrupted or challenged publicly

- Feeling dismissed or unacknowledged

- Encountering unpredictable or chaotic behavior

- Receiving unexpected criticism or rejection

- Wanting to impress or prove yourself

These are the pressure points where your masculine composure is tested. The world is not going to adjust for you. You must train your nervous system to remain grounded regardless of circumstance.

Powerful men don't seek to avoid discomfort—they learn to stay composed within it.

◆ Techniques for Regulating in the Moment

Here are strategies to stay calm, clear, and composed in any social dynamic:

1. **Name the emotion silently**

    When tension rises, label it internally: "I feel irritated." "I feel slighted." Naming deactivates the emotion's grip on you and puts you in the observer role.

2. **Slow your breath**

    Breathe deeply and slowly through your nose. Slow breathing tells your body you are safe—even when your ego feels threatened.

3. **Relax your face and jaw**

Most tension shows up in micro-expressions. Soften your face. Keep a neutral, steady gaze. A man who looks calm under fire is hard to provoke—and hard to ignore.

4. **Take space without retreating**

If emotion spikes, don't react impulsively. Pause. Use silence as a weapon. Let the tension breathe. It shows strength—not hesitation.

5. **Anchor to your values, not your ego**

Ask: *What would the man I'm becoming do right now?* Respond from principle, not pride.

◆ Becoming the Emotional Leader in the Room

In social dynamics, the most emotionally regulated person is the **true leader**, whether they hold a title or not. Others begin to match your tone, pace, and state—even subconsciously.

This is emotional dominance—but without aggression. It's the calm that:

- Defuses arguments

- Gains respect in silence

- Establishes authority without posturing

- Creates a sense of safety and certainty

People trust the man who doesn't flinch. They confide in the man who doesn't panic. They follow the man who doesn't need to escalate to be heard.

Final Thoughts: Power Is Calm in Motion

A man's emotional discipline is one of the deepest signals of his internal power. In a world of hyper-reactivity and overstimulation, your steadiness becomes a source of gravity.

Emotional regulation doesn't make you passive. It makes you **potent**. When others lose their cool, you remain composed. When people push, you don't break. When tension rises, you become the still point in the chaos.

That's influence. That's leadership. That's masculine frame.

Framing the Narrative and Setting the Tone

In every social interaction, a narrative is unfolding—and someone is setting the tone. The question is: **are you shaping that reality, or passively reacting to it?**

The man with masculine frame doesn't just walk into conversations. He walks in with **presence**, and that presence starts to shape the **story others are living in**. Influence, at its highest form, is not about controlling people. It's about guiding their **focus, assumptions, and expectations**—without forcing it.

This is called **framing the narrative**. And when done with calm strength, it becomes one of the most powerful tools a man can wield.

◆ What Is "Framing"?

A frame is the **unspoken lens through which people interpret a situation**. Whoever sets the frame, **sets the rules of engagement**—what matters, what's funny, what's serious, what's acceptable, what's possible.

In every interaction, someone's frame will dominate. If it's not yours, it will be someone else's—often shaped by fear, insecurity, or chaos. When you walk into a room without a solid internal frame, you get absorbed into theirs.

Framing is not about deception—it's about **direction**. It is the calm, intentional leadership of a conversation, mood, or mindset.

Tone: The Emotional Foundation of Influence

Setting the tone is how you **anchor the emotional state** of a situation. Tone is felt before words are processed. It determines whether others feel tense or relaxed, curious or guarded, elevated or defensive.

You set tone with:

- Your **first words** ("Let's slow this down" vs. "What's the problem here?")

- Your **vocal cadence** (Slow, steady, grounded speech equals authority.)

- Your **body language** (Open posture and eye contact signal safety and control.)

- Your **emotional state** (People feel your energy before they hear your intent.)

You don't just walk into a conversation—you bring a climate with you. Choose it.

Framing Examples in Practice

Let's look at real-world examples of frame and tone in action:

1. **In Conflict:**

    Weak frame: "Why are you doing this to me?"

    Strong frame: "Let's figure out what's really happening here."

    → The strong frame shifts the energy from blame to leadership.

2. **In Business:**

    Weak frame: "I hope this is okay with you..."

    Strong frame: "Here's the plan I recommend based on what matters most."

    → The strong frame establishes authority and direction.

3. **In Dating:**

Weak frame: "Do you like me?"

Strong frame: "We'll know if this connection is right with time."
→ The strong frame communicates non-neediness and grounded confidence.

Frames can be **reframed** at any moment—but it takes calm, unshaken composure and **belief in your perspective**.

◆ How to Hold Your Frame

It's not enough to present a strong frame—you must **hold it** when challenged. That's when real influence begins.

To hold your frame:

- **Don't explain excessively.** Over-explaining is often the death of strong tone. Say less, mean more.

- **Stay rooted emotionally.** The second you get defensive, you've lost the frame. Stay calm. Let others react—you don't have to.

- **Return to the truth.** Anchoring in your values, purpose, or principles reinforces your narrative. You're not "spinning" reality—you're standing in a more grounded one.

- **Use silence.** A pause can do more than a paragraph. It suggests certainty. Let your words settle. Let your presence speak.

◆ Leading the Narrative Ethically

Framing is powerful, and with that power comes responsibility. This is not about manipulating outcomes to serve your ego—it's about **creating clarity, calm, and leadership where there is chaos or confusion**.

When you frame a conversation, you're doing one of two things:

- Elevating the interaction into something more intentional and productive

- Or steering it to serve your fear, pride, or insecurity

Masculine frame chooses the former. You lead not by controlling others, but by controlling your own presence—and offering a stronger, more grounded narrative that others can trust.

Final Thoughts: You Are the Lens

Reality is not static. In every room, people are waiting for someone to define **what this is** and **how we're going to relate**. The man with masculine frame is the one who defines it—not through force, but through **internal clarity**.

You don't just walk into situations hoping they go well. You **shape them**, subtly and powerfully—by framing the story, setting the tone, and holding your calm, assertive presence until others align with it. This is what it means to lead the room before you say a word.

Influence as a By-Product of Integrity

Influence is often misunderstood. Many chase it like a prize—trying to say the right thing, impress the right people, or game social dynamics in their favor. But influence that must be chased is never real. It's conditional. Fragile. Performative.

The most powerful and lasting influence isn't something you do. It's something you become. It is the natural by-product of integrity.

When who you are, what you believe, and how you act are in alignment, people feel it—immediately. They may not be able to explain it, but they trust it. That trust is the foundation of influence.

Integrity is the invisible spine of masculine frame. Without it, everything collapses. With it, you don't have to posture, persuade, or pressure—you simply lead by being whole.

◆ Why Integrity Is Magnetic

Integrity means your inner world and outer world match. Your values are not theoretical—they show up in your actions. Your words are not empty—they are backed by evidence in how you live. You don't need to declare who you are. People can feel it.

This internal alignment generates a kind of silent credibility:

- You say little, but it carries weight.

- You make decisions without seeking approval.

- You move with purpose, not performance.

This kind of presence builds unspoken influence. People trust you not because you ask them to—but because they know where you stand, and they know you stand there regardless of who's watching.

◆ The Cost of Compromise

Every time you act out of alignment with your truth—whether to impress, avoid conflict, or gain approval—you fracture your frame. And over time, those small compromises erode both your influence and your self-respect.

Inconsistent men may win short-term attention, but they never earn long-term trust. And influence without trust is manipulation. It never lasts. A man who compromises to gain favor may be liked—but he'll never be followed.

A man who lives in integrity may be misunderstood—but he becomes a pillar others lean on when the world shakes.

◆ Living in Integrity: The Foundations

To make influence a natural extension of your character, start with these principles:

1. **Know your values—and live them in small decisions**

    Integrity starts when no one's watching. Every time you align your actions with your code, your spine strengthens.

2. **Say what you mean, and mean what you say**

    Let your words be an extension of your character, not a tool of convenience. Under-promise, over-deliver.

3. **Keep your boundaries—even when it's uncomfortable**

    Integrity often requires discomfort. But the man who avoids discomfort eventually becomes a slave to it.

4. **Don't explain your integrity—embody it**

    You don't need to justify your standards. You only need to live them. Let others adapt or exit.

5. **Clean up what you break**

    Integrity isn't perfection. You will slip. What matters is your willingness to own it, correct it, and return to center without self-pity.

♦ Influence as a Mirror

People are not influenced by your image. They're influenced by their reflection in your presence. When you live in integrity, others begin to ask more of themselves—not because you told them to, but because you showed them what alignment looks like.

You become a mirror. Not of their insecurities—but of their higher self. And that is the deepest influence there is.

Final Thoughts: Let Your Life Speak

When your life is aligned with your words, you don't need to "build influence." You become influential.

The steel spine of a man is forged in his principles. His calm heart is shaped by his ability to live them—especially when it's hard. Especially when no one claps for it.

This is integrity. This is influence. And this is the quiet force the world respects—even when it doesn't fully understand it.

10

Leading from the Core - Leadership

Leadership Beyond Words

Leadership is not a title. It's not charisma. It's not clever speeches, loud declarations, or telling others what to do. The deepest form of leadership is **wordless**.

It's how you move. How you respond under pressure. How you carry yourself when no one is watching—and especially when everyone is.

Leadership beyond words is about becoming a **living reference point**. A man so aligned with his values, so grounded in his presence, that others naturally **rise** in his company—not because he told them to, but because he showed them how.

True leadership doesn't come from commanding attention. It comes from **embodying stability**.

◆ The Silent Authority of Presence

Before you speak a word, you've already communicated everything others need to know about your leadership.

Your **tone, posture, energy, and stillness** create the frame people respond to.

- Do you radiate calm when others are losing their center?

- Do your eyes say "I'm grounded" before your mouth says anything at all?

- Do you create a felt sense of direction, even in silence?

People don't follow leaders because they talk more. They follow the ones whose **energy carries weight**. The man who leads from his core doesn't need to over-explain, over-promise, or over-perform. His presence says: *We're good. Follow me.*

◆ Alignment Speaks Louder Than Rhetoric

Words are cheap. Alignment is rare. The most respected leaders are those whose **behavior consistently matches their message**. That's how trust is built—not in the moments of public inspiration, but in the small private choices made with integrity.

When your team, your family, your circle sees that your standards don't change based on who's around—you become a pillar. Reliable. Predictable in the best way. Grounded even when things fall apart. Your leadership becomes **evident, not advertised**.

◆ Leading in Crisis Without a Speech

Leadership is tested most not in peace, but in pressure. When people panic, they don't need more information—they need **emotional grounding**. They look for the person who hasn't lost his head. The one whose breath is still slow, whose posture is still tall, whose decisions are made with clarity, not chaos.

In these moments:

- A nod carries more than a paragraph.

- A pause creates more reassurance than rushed reassurance.

- A calm "We've got this" from the right man is worth more than a thousand hyped-up orders.

This is the difference between noise and **leadership gravity**. And gravity is silent.

◆ Leadership as Energy Management

At its core, leadership is about managing energy—your own first, and then others'. You regulate your internal state so others can co-regulate through you. You remain the still point in the storm, giving others permission to **breathe, re-center, and move forward**.

Leadership beyond words is not passive. It's intentional, powerful, and deeply relational. It's felt in:

- How you enter a room

- How you handle disrespect

- How you listen

- How you don't flinch when others do

It's what happens when you **stop trying to perform leadership**, and start living it—calmly, consistently, and without the need for applause.

Final Thoughts: Let Them Feel It

The men who leave the deepest legacy aren't always the ones who spoke the most—they're the ones who lived in such alignment that their presence made others better. Real leadership isn't about what you say. It's about what others **feel called to become** in your presence.

So speak if the moment calls for it. But know this:

The man who **doesn't need words to lead** is the one people will listen to most when he finally speaks.

Inspiring Loyalty, not Just Obedience

Obedience is transactional. Loyalty is transformational. One lasts until pressure shows up. The other strengthens under fire.

Any man with a title, a louder voice, or a threat can extract obedience. But it takes a far deeper kind of leadership to inspire loyalty—a connection that isn't based on fear, but on respect, trust, and alignment.

Loyalty isn't commanded. It's earned through presence, consistency, and the quiet power of a man who lives his values even when no one's clapping.

◆ The Difference Between Obedience and Loyalty

Obedience sounds like: "I'll do what he says so I don't get in trouble."

Loyalty sounds like:

"I'll follow that man because I believe in how he moves."

Obedience is rooted in compliance. Loyalty is rooted in commitment.

The first vanishes when the incentives disappear. The second remains—even in difficulty, even when no one is watching. If you want to lead with masculine frame, your goal is not to make people submit. It's to become the kind of man others want to walk beside, because your presence calls them to something higher.

◆ How Loyalty Is Earned

There are three unshakable foundations of loyalty. Each one requires inner work before outer results.

1. **Consistency Over Time**

    People are watching you even when they say nothing. They notice how you respond under pressure, how you treat others when it's inconvenient, and whether your word holds weight.

    The more predictable your principles, the more dependable you become.

2. **Courageous Integrity**

    Loyalty forms around a man who tells the truth—especially when it's hard to hear. The man who doesn't bend his values to avoid conflict becomes the rare one people trust to stand with when things get real.

3. **Mutual Respect, Not Superiority**

    People don't give loyalty to those who look down on them. They give it to leaders who see their strength, expect the best from them, and walk with them—not above them. A grounded leader raises others up without shrinking himself.

◆ Loyalty Through Emotional Leadership

Loyalty isn't just intellectual—it's emotional. People become loyal when they feel:

- Safe in your presence (You don't blow up or collapse.)

- Seen for who they are and what they bring

- Supported through accountability, not enabling

- Challenged to grow by someone who's already doing the work

This means you lead not just with vision, but with emotional presence. You don't ask for loyalty—you create the conditions where it becomes inevitable.

◆ **What Kills Loyalty**

Many men sabotage loyalty without realizing it. Here's how:

- Inconsistency: Saying one thing, doing another

- Ego: Leading to be admired, not to serve or elevate

- Control: Micromanaging, overcorrecting, or leading through fear

- Lack of Empathy: Failing to understand the needs, drives, or realities of those you lead

The man who always has to remind others that he's the leader is the one least secure in his leadership. True leaders don't have to force loyalty. They cultivate it, through strength, stability, and earned respect.

Final Thoughts: Loyalty Reflects Leadership

The loyalty you receive is a mirror of the leadership you give. Not the leadership you preach—but the leadership you embody. Daily. Quietly. Unshakably.

People don't follow perfection. They follow consistency. They follow truth. They follow the man who stands tall when others fold, who speaks with conviction when the moment matters, and who lives in such alignment that loyalty is the natural response.

You don't need to chase it. Become it. And let them come to you.

Strategic Thinking and Presence

Strategic thinking isn't just about **outsmarting opponents** or planning your next move. It's about seeing the **bigger picture, understanding long-term consequences,** and making decisions with a calm, grounded awareness of where you are and where you want to go.

But none of this can be achieved without **presence**. In fact, true strategic thinking emerges from a place of **mental stillness and emotional clarity**. The stronger your frame, the clearer your strategic vision becomes.

Strategic thinking and presence are two sides of the same coin. You can't afford to think ahead without first being present in the moment. You can't lead others if you're constantly caught in short-term reactions. The man with a steel spine and a calm heart **sees more clearly**, plans with greater precision, and acts with **purpose**—because he is **rooted in the now**.

◆ The Power of Present-Moment Awareness

Strategic thinking starts with a **deep awareness** of the present moment. You can't lead effectively if you're not aware of the ground beneath your feet. Every move you make should be **rooted** in the situation you're facing right now—not just in what you want the outcome to be.

Being present allows you to:

- **Read the dynamics** of any situation—whether it's a conversation, a negotiation, or a challenge.

- **Calibrate your response** based on the real-time information you have, not assumptions or emotional reactions.

- **Make thoughtful decisions** rather than rash ones driven by stress or urgency.

When you're present, you're not just reacting—you're **leading with clarity** and **purpose**.

◆ Strategic Thinking: Moving from Reaction to Action

Many people live in a state of constant reaction, bouncing from one crisis to the next. A true leader, however, cultivates the ability to **think strategically** even when surrounded by chaos.

Strategic thinking requires you to step back and evaluate:

- **What's the long-term impact of my decisions?**

- **What is the larger goal I'm trying to achieve?**

- **What are the patterns and opportunities I can leverage in this moment?**

It's not about knowing every move before you make it. It's about having the **awareness** and **patience** to wait for the right moment, the right opportunity, and then acting decisively when it's time to move.

When you take a step back from the immediate pressures of a situation, you give yourself the **space to think**. The man who thinks with clarity, grounded in the present moment, is far more effective than the one who is ruled by short-term impulses.

◆ The Quiet Force of Thoughtful Action

Presence and strategy converge in action. It's not just what you think—it's what you **do** that sets you apart as a leader.

But here's the thing: the most strategic actions aren't always the loudest or most obvious. The most powerful decisions are often made in **quiet moments** of reflection. Strategic thinking leads to **decisive actions**—actions that are measured, considered, and deeply aligned with your values and goals.

You don't need to announce your moves or justify them constantly. When your decisions are rooted in strategic thinking and made with clarity of mind, your presence speaks louder than any explanation. The right actions at the right time, with the right people, have an impact that lasts.

◆ Strategic Leadership: The Role of Patience

A true strategic thinker doesn't rush. He doesn't force outcomes. He is **patient**, understanding that some moves take time to unfold. His presence allows others to be patient with him as well.

Patience in leadership means:

- **Knowing when to act, and when to wait.**

- **Resisting the urge to fill silence with unnecessary noise.**

- **Trusting the process, even when the results aren't immediate.**

A leader who rushes is often acting from a place of fear, not strategy. Strategic thinking demands a **calm resolve**—the understanding that the best results are often cultivated over time, and that **hasty decisions** often lead to unnecessary consequences.

Aligning Strategy with Values

Strategic thinking isn't just about winning—it's about winning in a way that **aligns with your values** and **sustains long-term success**. A true leader doesn't take shortcuts or compromise principles for the sake of expediency. Every move, every decision should reflect your core beliefs.

When your strategy is rooted in integrity and a clear sense of purpose, your actions become more powerful. They inspire others not just to follow, but to **believe in** what you're doing. People want to follow leaders who make decisions based on what's right, not what's easy.

Final Thoughts: Lead with Clarity, Move with Purpose

Strategic thinking is a product of **calm presence**. It's the result of a man who isn't caught in the hustle, the noise, or the urgency of the moment. He **sees clearly**, acts decisively, and leads with an unshakable sense of purpose.

The best leaders think strategically, but their strategy is always rooted in **presence**—the kind of presence that can see the big picture, make tough decisions with confidence, and act with integrity in every situation.

When you lead from the core, you don't just lead in the moment. You shape the future. And the clarity, patience, and decisiveness you embody create the space for others to **follow with trust** and **respect**.

How Masculine Frame Shapes Group Dynamics

The energy of a group is often determined by the frame of its leader. Just as a man with a strong, grounded masculine frame exudes quiet authority and presence, so too does his energy influence the dynamics of those around him. Whether in a workplace, a family, or a social circle, your frame dictates the tone, flow, and interaction of the group.

Masculine frame doesn't demand control—it invites respect, and in doing so, it creates an environment where others naturally follow the leader's example. Group dynamics shift when the leader stands firm in his convictions, manages his energy, and remains calm under pressure.

In this section, we'll explore how a man's composure, authority, and presence shape the behavior, energy, and cohesiveness of the groups he leads, whether formally or informally.

◆ The Center of Calm

A masculine frame brings a centered energy to any group. When a man remains grounded, calm, and in control of his emotions, he sets the emotional tone for the group. The stronger his frame, the more others are likely to mirror his composure, creating a ripple effect that stabilizes the group.

When uncertainty, tension, or stress arises within a group, people naturally look to the leader for guidance—consciously or unconsciously. The leader who is unshaken, whose body language and voice exude certainty, creates an invisible force field of confidence that helps others calm down and re-center.

A group feels safe when the leader remains consistent, present, and unwavering, even in moments of pressure. The group's emotional stability depends on the leader's ability to anchor the energy. Without this center, chaos can creep in, causing friction, confusion, and a breakdown in cooperation.

◆ Unspoken Authority: The Power of Presence

In group dynamics, authority doesn't have to be loud or assertive. In fact, the most powerful leaders don't force their authority—they embody it through their silent confidence. Their presence alone commands respect, creating an environment where others naturally defer to them.

When a man stands tall in his masculine frame, he doesn't need to constantly remind others of his position or qualifications. His mere presence speaks volumes. Body language, eye contact, and posture convey a message far more powerful than words: *"I am the leader here, and I am secure in that."*

This silent authority fosters trust. It removes the need for over-explaining or justifying decisions. It encourages autonomy within the group, as the leader's clarity and confidence give others the permission to take ownership of their roles and responsibilities.

◆ Setting the Tone for Respect and Accountability

A masculine frame shapes the respect and accountability in a group by establishing clear boundaries and expectations—without needing to enforce them through aggression or micromanagement. When the leader consistently maintains his standards and refuses to tolerate disrespect, the group begins to internalize these boundaries.

- Respect becomes non-negotiable because the leader models it.

- Accountability becomes ingrained because the leader is dependable, fair, and consistent.

When the leader's words align with his actions, when he holds himself to the same standards he holds others to, the group begins to follow suit. The masculine frame isn't about exerting control over others—it's about fostering mutual respect. The leader's example of integrity and consistency naturally encourages others to step up, follow through, and support one another.

Inspiring Trust and Cooperation

Masculine frame fosters trust within the group by demonstrating reliability and strength in action. In groups where the leader's frame is solid, trust grows organically—because people sense that the leader is stable and that his decisions come from a place of wisdom and clarity.

In such an environment:

- Members feel empowered to contribute without fear of ridicule or judgment.

- Team members feel psychologically safe to take calculated risks and step outside their comfort zones.

- Trust leads to greater cooperation, which in turn fosters stronger collaboration, innovative ideas, and higher morale.

A leader with a strong masculine frame doesn't need to micromanage, because the sense of trust that permeates the group eliminates the need for constant supervision. Autonomy within a framework of trust leads to better results and greater collective success.

Encouraging Leadership in Others

A strong masculine frame doesn't just shape group dynamics by imposing order or maintaining authority. It also inspires others to take ownership and initiative. A true leader doesn't just lead by example—he encourages others to step into their own leadership as well.

When others feel the strength of the leader's frame, they often rise to the occasion. The leader creates a culture of leadership, where every individual feels empowered to lead within their capacity, whether in a project, a decision-making process, or in their personal development.

By showing strength, clarity, and integrity, the leader with a solid masculine frame cultivates an environment of growth and empowerment. Rather than suppressing the voices and abilities of others, he magnifies their potential, encouraging them to stand strong in their own truth.

Final Thoughts: Mastering Group Dynamics

When a man leads with a strong masculine frame, his presence isn't just felt by those around him—it shapes the behavior and emotional atmosphere of the entire group. People will follow his example because he doesn't just give orders—he becomes the standard.

Through clarity, calmness, and integrity, the leader with a masculine frame shapes group dynamics by fostering a culture of respect, trust, and accountability. His presence calms turbulence, his authority inspires loyalty, and his consistency creates a foundation upon which others can thrive.

In every group dynamic, whether in business, relationships, or communities, the strength of the masculine frame is the cornerstone for building high-functioning, cooperative, and resilient teams. The stronger the frame, the more the group will rise to meet its potential—because the leader sets the tone and guides with quiet power.

11

The Real You - Authenticity

Why Fake Confidence Fails

In a world obsessed with appearances, it's easy to fall into the trap of **faking confidence**. After all, we live in a culture where the **outward projection of success** often gets more attention than the real substance behind it. It's tempting to wear the armor of fake confidence: standing tall, speaking loudly, and projecting an image of invulnerability.

But here's the truth: **fake confidence is fragile**, and it's only a matter of time before it shatters under pressure. People can sense when confidence is an act, and sooner or later, the cracks will show.

The reason fake confidence fails is simple: it's **inauthentic**. True confidence isn't about posing or pretending. It's about **self-assurance**, which comes from a place of deep-rooted authenticity. When you lead with authenticity, you are secure enough to show your true self, flaws and all, and still maintain your strength. **That's the kind of confidence that endures**—the kind that others feel and respect.

◆ The Problem with Pretending

When you put on a mask of confidence, it's like trying to build a house on sand. **Pretending to be someone you're not** takes a tremendous amount of energy. You're constantly worried about how you're being perceived, what others might think, and whether or not you're "pulling it off." This creates a **disconnect** between how you feel on the inside and how you're acting on the outside.

People pick up on this incongruity. While they may not consciously understand why they don't fully trust you, they can sense the tension and discomfort. It becomes clear that what they're seeing is a **performance**, not a real person. And no matter how polished your "act" is, it can't hide the **vulnerability** underneath.

Fake confidence also tends to be **reactive**, often fueled by external validation—such as approval from others, the need for admiration, or fear of rejection. This makes it **unstable** and easily broken. You might feel confident in one situation, but as soon as someone challenges your authority or questions your worth, your carefully constructed facade crumbles.

True confidence, however, isn't dependent on external sources. It is rooted in the **quiet understanding** that you are enough, just as you are. It doesn't need to perform—it just **is**.

◆ The Dangers of Living in a Shell

Living in a shell of fake confidence limits your ability to connect with others on a deep level. **Authentic relationships** require vulnerability—the willingness to be seen for who you truly are, imperfections and all. When you're constantly hiding behind a mask of confidence, you deny yourself the chance to form real, meaningful connections.

People are drawn to authenticity. When they sense **genuineness** in someone, they feel safe. They feel like they can lower their guards and let down their facades, too. But when they sense a mask or facade, they will hold back, wary of the disconnect. This creates an invisible wall that prevents true emotional intimacy and mutual respect from forming.

Moreover, the longer you rely on fake confidence, the further you drift from the **real you**. Over time, you might lose touch with your true voice, your true values, and your true purpose. You may even forget why you started pretending in the first place.

Eventually, the strain of living a lie takes its toll. **The cracks in the mask** become more obvious, and you may find yourself unable to keep up the charade. The result? **Burnout**, frustration, and a sense of disconnection from yourself and others.

◆ Authentic Confidence: The Quiet Power of Being You

Authentic confidence doesn't require pretending to be someone else. It requires you to be **fully comfortable with yourself**—your strengths, your flaws, your ambitions, and your vulnerabilities.

Here's why authentic confidence works:

1. **It's rooted in self-awareness**: Authentic confidence is the product of knowing who you are—your values, your purpose, and your capabilities. It isn't about putting on an act. It's about standing tall in your own truth, no matter what others might think. When you're at peace with yourself, others can sense it.

2. **It's consistent**: Authentic confidence isn't fleeting. It doesn't disappear when you face a challenge or encounter criticism. Instead, it becomes a steady source of strength. When your confidence is grounded in authenticity, you **don't need validation** from others because your worth doesn't depend on their opinions.

3. **It invites respect, not admiration**: True confidence doesn't demand attention or admiration. It naturally draws respect. People are attracted to those who are self-assured but not arrogant—those who can stand firm without needing to boast. Authenticity is magnetic because it signals that you are secure in who you are, and that's a rare quality in a world full of facades.

4. **It fosters connection**: Authentic confidence allows others to feel comfortable being themselves around you. When you are real, others feel safe to be real with you. This creates an environment of **mutual respect and trust**, where relationships can flourish.

◆ How to Cultivate Authentic Confidence

Building authentic confidence doesn't happen overnight. It's a process of **self-discovery** and **self-acceptance**. Here are some key practices that will help you cultivate this deep, unshakeable confidence:

- **Embrace vulnerability**: Don't be afraid to show who you really are. Accept your flaws, your mistakes, and your imperfections as part of your unique story. The more you own your vulnerabilities, the more your confidence will grow.

- **Stop seeking external validation**: True confidence comes from within. Focus on aligning with your values and doing things that are meaningful to you, rather than seeking approval from others.

- **Be consistent in your actions**: Authenticity is built on consistency. Show up every day as your true self, and act in alignment with your beliefs. The more consistent you are, the more others will see your confidence as genuine and reliable.

- **Stop comparing yourself**: The trap of fake confidence often stems from comparing yourself to others. Let go of the need to compete or compare. Recognize that your journey is unique, and you have your own path to walk.

Final Thoughts: Confidence is the Quiet Power of the Real You

Fake confidence may win you temporary approval, but authentic confidence will win you the respect and loyalty of those who matter. It will create a life of deeper connection, richer experiences, and **lasting influence**.

When you're grounded in authenticity, you stop pretending. You stop performing. And in doing so, you become the most powerful version of yourself—a version that can weather storms, navigate challenges, and inspire others simply by being real.

Authentic confidence is not loud or brash. It's quiet, steady, and **unshakable**. And it's the only kind of confidence that will stand the test of time.

Inner Congruence = Outer Power

If your inner world is chaotic, no amount of performance can cover it up for long. If your inner world is aligned—calm, clear, and anchored—your presence alone becomes power.

This is the secret most men never discover:

Power doesn't come from posturing. It comes from congruence.

Inner congruence means your **thoughts, feelings, words, and actions** are in alignment. There's no internal war, no performance to maintain, no mask to hold up. What people see is what's real—and that's exactly why they trust it.

When a man is congruent, he becomes **undeniable**. He walks into a room and people feel his energy before he says a word. Why? Because there's no tension between who he is and how he shows up. That clarity is rare. That alignment is magnetic.

◆ **What Is Inner Congruence?**

Inner congruence is the **internal harmony** between your values, your identity, and your behavior.

It means:

- You believe what you say.

- You act in line with what you believe.

- You own your flaws without shame.

- You don't say "yes" when you mean "no."

- You speak truth even when it's inconvenient.

You're not performing—you're **living your truth**.

There's no gap between the man you are in private and the one you present in public. That alignment gives your words **weight**. It gives your silence **depth**. It gives your presence **power**.

◆ The Consequences of Incongruence

When you're out of alignment—when your words say one thing but your energy says another—people feel it. They may not be able to name it, but they'll sense it. And they'll **doubt** you because of it.

- If you pretend to be confident but carry insecurity in your tone, people will hesitate to trust you.

- If you talk about values but act in ways that betray them, people will keep their distance.

- If you try to lead but haven't led yourself first, people won't follow for long.

Incongruence creates tension. It's the subtle unease others feel in your presence, and it always erodes trust over time. You might be able to fake strength for a moment, but people will never trust what you haven't truly embodied. Real power comes from being **whole inside**—because then you no longer have anything to prove.

◆ Congruence Creates Influence

The most powerful leaders are not the loudest. They're the most **aligned**. When your values and behavior match, you become predictable—in the best way. People know what you stand for. They know what you'll tolerate and what you won't. They know your yes means yes, and your no means no.

That clarity builds **trust**. And trust is the foundation of all influence.

- In relationships, it means others can lean on you emotionally without fear of hidden agendas.

- In leadership, it means people follow you not because they have to, but because they **believe in you**.

- In life, it means you move through the world with quiet power—**centered**, unshakeable, and deeply respected.

◆ Cultivating Inner Congruence

Congruence isn't a gift—it's a **discipline**. It's forged through deep reflection and relentless honesty.

Here are practices to help build it:

1. **Clarify your values**

   Know what you stand for. Define your core principles. Without this, you can't align with anything meaningful.

2. **Audit your actions**

   Where are you living out of alignment? What habits, relationships, or compromises are weakening your integrity? Clean them up.

3. **Speak your truth**

   Don't say what sounds good—say what's **real**. Train yourself to be honest without being harsh. The more your words reflect your inner truth, the more powerful they become.

4. **Close the gap**

   Congruence doesn't mean perfection. It means **integrity in motion**. When you fall short, acknowledge it. Own it. Course correct quickly.

Final Thoughts: Power Without Performance

Masculine frame isn't about image—it's about **alignment**. It's the quiet strength of a man who has reconciled who he is with how he lives. That man doesn't need to perform. He doesn't need to chase validation or manage perception. He just **is**. And that's enough. When your inner world is aligned, your outer world bends to match it.

That's the equation:

Inner congruence = outer power.

Removing the Masks of Insecurity

Every man wears masks at some point in his life. Some are subtle—like the easy joke that hides discomfort. Others are heavy—like the loud bravado meant to cover fear, or the "nice guy" routine that hides resentment. All of them stem from the same place: **insecurity**.

Insecurity whispers, "You're not enough as you are." And in response, you build a persona. A mask. Something you hope the world will accept, admire, or at least not reject.

But here's the truth:

Every mask you wear distances you from your real power.

Masculine frame begins where masks end. The moment you drop the performance and show up as **yourself—raw, real, and steady—that's when your presence becomes unforgettable.**

◆ The Roots of the Mask

Men learn early on to hide vulnerability. Maybe you were told to "man up," "don't cry," "never show weakness." So, you did what boys do—you adapted. You built walls. You projected confidence, charm, or control—even when you didn't feel it. You put on a mask, not to deceive, but to survive.

But survival mode isn't living—it's **performing**. That mask may have gotten you through hard times. But now, it keeps you **small**. It prevents you from forming real connections. It keeps your true power—the kind that can't be faked—**trapped beneath layers of performance**.

◆ The Cost of the Mask

The longer you wear the mask, the harder it is to remember who you really are underneath.

- You might be liked, but you won't be **respected**.

- You might impress people, but you won't **inspire** them.

- You might be surrounded by others, but feel completely **alone**.

Wearing a mask means constantly managing perception. It's exhausting. It's fragile. And deep down, you know it's not sustainable. Because when you're not being real, every compliment feels hollow, every success feels unearned, and every relationship feels conditional.

And perhaps most dangerously, the mask numbs you to your own **inner truth**—your real values, your honest emotions, your unfiltered voice.

◆ Taking the Mask Off: The Shift into Strength

Removing the mask isn't about exposure. It's about **liberation**. It doesn't mean you share every feeling or expose every wound. It means you stop **pretending**. You stop chasing approval, and instead start living in alignment with your **real self**.

This is the turning point where insecurity transforms into **integrity**.

- When you stop hiding your fear, you gain **courage**.

- When you stop faking your competence, you gain **confidence through action**.

- When you stop seeking validation, you begin building **self-respect**.

Dropping the mask is uncomfortable at first—but what replaces it is **real power**. Quiet. Centered. Undeniable.

◆ How to Drop the Mask

Here's how you begin reclaiming yourself:

1. **Identify the masks you wear**

    Do you act like the funny guy to deflect seriousness? Do you overcompensate with arrogance? Do you say "yes" when you want to say "no"? Start noticing when you're being performative instead of honest.

2. **Ask what fear drives the mask**

    Every mask hides something: fear of rejection, fear of failure, fear of being seen as weak. Name it. When you face the fear head-on, it loses its grip.

3. **Practice grounded honesty**

    Speak more from truth than performance. Start small—say how you really feel in safe spaces. Let your "no" be a no. Let your boundaries stand firm. Let your presence be enough.

4. **Surround yourself with realness**

    Stop investing energy in relationships where you have to wear a mask. Be around people who value authenticity over image. Your environment either reinforces your mask—or encourages your truth.

Final Thoughts: The Man Behind the Mask

You are not your mask. You are not your past. You are not the image you think the world wants. You are a man with depth, power, and presence—and none of that needs to be **proven**. It just needs to be **reclaimed**.

When you remove the mask, you allow your **masculine frame to breathe**. You stop filtering your essence. You start commanding respect without ever asking for it. And you realize that the strength you were trying to fake… was inside you all along.

Take off the mask. Stand in your truth. That's where the real man begins.

Telling the Truth Without Apology

There's a difference between being honest and being unapologetically truthful. Many men tell the truth with disclaimers, softeners, or back-pedalling built in.

"I don't mean to sound harsh, but…"

"Sorry if this comes off the wrong way…"

"Just my opinion, but…"

These are pre-emptive apologies for having a spine. Why? Because we're conditioned to believe that truth is only acceptable if it's wrapped in comfort. But truth—raw, grounded truth—isn't always comfortable. And that's precisely what makes it powerful.

When a man speaks his truth without apology, he signals certainty, integrity, and self-respect. He's not rude. He's not aggressive. He's simply rooted in what is real. This is one of the most defining traits of masculine frame: the calm, clear, unapologetic expression of truth.

◆ Truth Is Not Cruelty

Let's be clear: telling the truth without apology doesn't mean being blunt or disrespectful. It's not about dropping truth bombs and walking away. It's about clarity without performance, honesty without fear, and assertiveness without ego.

Apologizing for your truth dilutes its power and undermines your frame. When you second-guess your words mid-sentence or sugarcoat your beliefs to avoid discomfort, you're signaling that you don't fully stand behind what you're saying.

A man in his frame doesn't speak to be liked. He speaks because what he says is aligned with who he is. That's what makes it compelling. That's what earns trust.

◆ Why We Apologize for the Truth

The need to soften the truth often comes from fear—fear of conflict, disapproval, or being labeled as difficult. But when you dilute your message to avoid discomfort, you sacrifice your integrity.

Here's what's really happening when you apologize for your truth:

- You make other people's comfort more important than your honesty.

- You teach yourself to filter your expression instead of developing clarity and emotional maturity.

- You give away power and weaken your presence.

When you habitually apologize for your truth, you train people to expect hesitation from you. And hesitant men aren't trusted, followed, or respected for long.

◆ Speaking from the Center

The key to telling the truth without apology is speaking from your center, not your emotions. Truth spoken from ego is harsh. Truth spoken from fear is weak. But truth spoken from grounded certainty? That's leadership.

Here's what that looks like in practice:

- You say what you mean—no more, no less.

- You maintain a steady tone, eye contact, and calm energy.

- You don't rush. You don't explain too much. You let your words land.

- You don't fold under awkward silence or pushback.

- You don't need everyone to agree—you just need to stand firm.

This kind of truth doesn't provoke defensiveness because it's not a weapon—it's a mirror. It reflects reality. And most people, deep down, are craving that level of clarity in a world drowning in noise and spin.

◆ **Practice: Building the Truth Muscle**

Like any strength, unapologetic truth-telling is developed with conscious practice:

1. Start small – Practice expressing your real opinion in low-stakes conversations. Don't agree to be polite. Speak honestly and observe how people respond.

2. Drop the disclaimers – Eliminate "just," "maybe," "I think," "sorry but…" from your sentences. These weaken your authority. Replace them with clarity and pause.

3. Own your words – Say it like you mean it. Not louder—firmer. Your tone should match the weight of your words.

4. Learn to sit in silence – After speaking truth, don't fill the space. Let your words do their work. Trust their impact. Let others process.

Final Thoughts: Truth Is a Leadership Trait

Telling the truth without apology isn't about dominance. It's about alignment.

It says:

"I know who I am. I know what I see. And I'm willing to stand in that truth, even if it's uncomfortable." This doesn't make you difficult—it makes you dependable. It doesn't make you harsh—it makes you clear. And in a world full of noise, clarity is rare power.

Speak with honesty. Speak with conviction. Speak without apology. Not to control anyone—but because you refuse to betray yourself.

12

Solid Ground – Becoming Grounded

Centering Practices for Stability

In a chaotic, fast-moving world, a grounded man is a rare force. He's not easily swayed by moods, opinions, or the emotional storms of others. He doesn't overreact, overcompensate, or over-speak. He responds instead of reacts, and when he moves, people feel it.

This groundedness doesn't come from luck. It comes from practice—daily habits that build internal stillness, emotional control, and unshakable presence. To be grounded is to be centered in yourself. When your mind, breath, and body are aligned, your masculine frame becomes undeniable.

Below are powerful centering practices to help you root yourself in stillness and clarity—so you stop floating through life and start standing firm in it.

◆ 1. The Power of the Breath

Your breath is your anchor. When your emotions are high, your breath is shallow. When your mind races, your breath becomes erratic. But when you slow and deepen your breath, your nervous system stabilizes. You return to the present moment.

Practice:

- Box Breathing: Inhale for 4 seconds, hold for 4, exhale for 4, hold for 4. Repeat for 2–5 minutes.

- Grounding Breath: Inhale deeply through the nose, expanding the diaphragm. Exhale slowly through the mouth while focusing on your feet pressing into the ground.

Make breathwork a part of your daily rhythm—especially before high-stakes conversations, decisions, or moments where your frame could be tested.

◆ 2. Body Awareness and Posture

Your body reflects your mind. A grounded man has presence in his posture: shoulders relaxed but strong, feet planted, jaw unclenched, eyes steady. When you bring awareness to your physical stance, you instantly shift your internal state.

Practice:

- Do regular body scans—mentally move your attention from head to toe, releasing tension from each part.

- Stand with both feet firmly on the floor for 60 seconds each morning, feeling your weight distribute evenly.

- Use "Posture Check" prompts on your phone throughout the day: head up, chest open, spine long.

Why it works: When your body is aligned, your emotions follow. People instinctively respect a man who stands still, tall, and relaxed under pressure.

◆ 3. Mental Stillness Rituals

Your frame is only as strong as your mental clarity. A scattered mind leaks power. Grounded men cultivate inner stillness through daily mental discipline.

Practice:

- 5-Minute Stillness: Sit in silence with no phone, music, or stimulus. Simply observe your thoughts without judgment. The goal isn't to stop them—but to detach from them.

- Nature Walks (No Tech): Leave your devices. Walk slowly. Observe, breathe, feel. Let the natural world regulate your nervous system.

- Journaling for Clarity: Spend 10 minutes writing freely—dump your worries, questions, or conflicts. Seeing them on paper helps you process and regain mental order.

When your mind is quiet, you begin to respond from conscious choice, not emotional impulse.

◆ 4. Emotional Check-Ins

Grounded men are not emotionless. They are simply unshaken by emotion. Stability comes from the ability to feel fully without being ruled by what you feel. This requires emotional intelligence: the awareness of what's happening within you, and the discipline to stay centered in it.

Practice:

- Throughout the day, ask:

"What am I feeling right now?"

"Where is this emotion in my body?"

"Can I sit with it without needing to fix or flee?"

This practice builds emotional maturity. You stop being surprised by your feelings—and start mastering them.

◆ 5. Create Daily Grounding Rituals

Stability is not a mindset—it's a habit. Rituals train the nervous system to expect calm, to seek center, to regulate without external validation.

Examples:

- Morning Ritual: Stretch, breathe, journal, and move—before checking your phone.

- Evening Ritual: Reflect, breathe, and slow your heart rate before bed. No screens, no stress.

- Moment Rituals: Before walking into a room, meeting, or conflict—pause, inhale deeply, and drop your awareness into your body.

These rituals train your body to associate presence with peace—and your peace becomes your power.

Final Thoughts: From Scattered to Solid

Most men chase power without realizing that power starts with stillness. Stillness is not weakness. It's not passivity. It's the root of all decisive action. When you are grounded, you become trustworthy—to yourself and to others. You move slower, but with greater impact. You speak less, but with greater weight. You lead not by force, but by presence.

These centering practices are not just techniques—they are the foundation of your masculine frame. Because a man who is anchored within cannot be pushed around by the world outside.

How to Stay Calm Under Fire

Every man is calm when the room is quiet, when he's rested, and when life is flowing smoothly. But the true test of masculine frame is what happens when pressure hits—when emotions flare, when you're being challenged, disrespected, or provoked.

Do you fold? Do you flare up? Or do you hold your center and move with clarity?

The man who can remain composed under fire becomes a natural leader. He commands respect without ever raising his voice. He holds space when others collapse. And in chaos, he becomes the calm force everyone instinctively looks to.

Calm under fire isn't natural—it's trained. It's the result of inner discipline, emotional regulation, and mental conditioning. Here's how to develop it.

◆ 1. Control the Breath, Control the Situation

The first casualty of stress is breath. When emotions rise, your breathing becomes short and shallow. This signals your nervous system to panic—even if there's no real threat. **Your breath is your override switch.**

When you slow your breathing, your heart rate drops. Your body calms. Your thoughts clear. You regain control—of yourself and of the moment.

Practice in the fire:

- Inhale slowly through your nose for 4 seconds.

- Hold for 2 seconds.

- Exhale through your mouth for 6–8 seconds.

- Repeat silently as you maintain eye contact and a calm demeanor.

This subtle act re-centers you without needing to speak or move. No one needs to know you're using it—but they'll feel the shift.

◆ 2. Master the Emotional Gap

Between stimulus and response lies a small space. Grounded men live in that space. They don't react impulsively—they **choose their response**.

When under fire—whether in an argument, confrontation, or high-pressure moment—your first instinct is rarely your strongest move. Emotional men react. Grounded men pause.

Build the gap by training yourself to ask:

- "What's actually happening right now?"

- "What outcome do I want here?"

- "Does this need a reaction—or just presence?"

You don't always need to speak. Sometimes the most powerful move is to hold your gaze, stay still, and let the moment pass through you without losing yourself in it.

◆ 3. Detach from Ego, Anchor in Values

Most men lose their composure when their ego gets hit—when they feel disrespected, overlooked, or attacked. They confuse emotional pain with a loss of identity. This is a trap.

You're not your emotions. You're not your reputation. You're not how others treat you. You are who you **choose to be**—especially under fire. The grounded man doesn't respond to preserve ego. He responds to uphold **values**.

Ask yourself:

- "Am I reacting to protect my pride—or to protect my principles?"

- "Will I still be proud of this response tomorrow?"

When you act from values, you act with **honor**, not just emotion. And others feel the difference.

◆ 4. Own the Energy in the Room

Fire doesn't always come from confrontation. Sometimes it's the heat of public pressure, difficult decisions, or emotional breakdowns around you. In those moments, grounded men don't shrink or overcompensate—they **own the room** with their stillness.

How?

- Keep your voice low and slow.

- Move deliberately.

- Maintain eye contact without staring down.

- Speak last, not first—listen before leading.

This type of calm changes the energy of the room. You become the anchor in the storm, the fixed point people subconsciously rally around.

◆ 5. Train in Discomfort Before It Matters

You can't stay calm under pressure if you only practice calm in comfort. You must **train your nervous system** to hold steady in tension.

Build your tolerance by choosing pressure daily:

- Cold showers or cold plunges (stay calm while breathing slowly)

- Intense physical training (focus on breath control, not just output)

- Crucial conversations (state your truth without flinching)

- Public speaking (speak slowly despite adrenaline)

Over time, your nervous system adapts. You stop flinching when tested. Your body learns that tension doesn't mean danger—it means **opportunity to lead**.

Final Thoughts: Be the Calm in the Chaos

Staying calm under fire isn't about being numb. It's about being **prepared**.

- When others yell, you speak low.

- When others blame, you take ownership.

- When others panic, you stay present.

- When the fire rises, you remain the mountain.

This is masculine frame in action—steel in the spine, calm in the heart. It's not just strength. It's strength others can count on.

Managing Anxiety, Overthinking and Emotional Triggers

There's a storm that can hit any man—quietly and without warning. It doesn't come from the outside world. It comes from **within**. Anxiety.

Overthinking. Emotional triggers that hijack your state before you even realize what's happening.

These internal storms erode your masculine frame faster than any external challenge ever could. They pull you out of the present, make your energy erratic, and cause you to second-guess your words, decisions, and even your worth.

But here's the truth:

You don't eliminate anxiety by trying to force it out. You manage it by learning to **anchor yourself through it**. A grounded man isn't free from emotional triggers—he's just not **owned** by them. Let's break down how you get there.

◆ 1. Understand the Root, Not Just the Reaction

Every overreaction is a **signal**—not a flaw. Every anxiety spiral, every emotional trigger, every restless loop in your mind is trying to say something. The key is not to fight the feeling, but to **decode it**.

Ask yourself:

- "What's the actual threat I feel here?"

- "Is this about now—or am I reacting from past pain?"

- "Am I afraid of losing control, approval, or certainty?"

Triggers aren't about the moment—they're about **meaning**. When you can spot the story behind the emotion, the power of that trigger starts to fade.

Awareness is always the first step to self-mastery.

◆ 2. Calm the Nervous System First, Think Later

You cannot outthink anxiety in an activated state. When you're emotionally triggered, your body shifts into **fight, flight, or freeze** mode. Blood leaves the thinking brain and rushes to the survival brain. That's why your thoughts loop, your chest tightens, and logic seems unreachable. Before you try to "solve" anything, you must **reset the body**.

Use this protocol:

- **Step outside** if possible (change your environment).

- Take 10 **slow, deliberate breaths**, longer on the exhale.

- Place both feet firmly on the floor and **feel your weight**.

- Put your hand on your chest and say, silently:

"I'm safe. I'm grounded. I choose how I respond."

Regulate first. Respond second. A man in control of his body is a man in control of his frame.

◆ 3. Break the Overthinking Loop

Overthinking is fear wearing a thinking mask. It's your mind trying to control the uncontrollable, solve the unsolvable, or predict the unpredictable. It creates motion without progress.

To break the loop, you need to **interrupt the cycle**:

- **Name it:** Say out loud (or write down), "I'm overthinking. This is a loop."

- **Move your body:** Take a walk, do pushups, stretch—anything to disrupt the mental tension.

- **Time-box the problem:** Set a 10-minute timer to think or journal about it. When the timer ends, so does the rumination.

- **Shift to action:** Ask, "What's one concrete action I can take right now to move forward?"

Overthinking thrives in inaction. Action restores your sense of control—and your grounded presence.

◆ 4. Reframe Triggers as Training

The goal isn't to avoid triggers. It's to **transform your relationship with them**. Every time you feel emotionally hijacked—by rejection, criticism, confrontation, or failure—you're being given an opportunity to strengthen your masculine core.

You can either:

- React emotionally, reinforce old patterns, and collapse your frame. **Or**

- Slow down, observe without judgment, and respond with intention.

Ask yourself:

- "What would the strongest version of me do in this moment?"

- "What lesson is this trigger inviting me to master?"

When you shift your perspective from "Why is this happening to me?" to "What is this building in me?"—you become unshakable.

◆ 5. Build Your Internal Baseline Daily

Staying grounded in high-stress moments depends on how you live when things are calm. Anxiety and overthinking often take over when you haven't built a solid internal rhythm.

This is why **daily practices matter**—they lower your baseline stress, sharpen your awareness, and keep your emotional bandwidth wide.

Anchor habits include:

- Morning silence or meditation

- Daily movement (weights, walks, breathwork)

- Intentional solitude (time without inputs: no phone, no noise)

- Sleep, hydration, nutrition—your physiology is the foundation

The more you **build stability into your life**, the less likely you are to spin out when tension hits.

Final Thoughts: Stillness Is a Skill

You won't stop life from testing you. You won't eliminate every anxious thought. And you'll still get triggered—it's part of being human. But what separates a reactive man from a grounded one is how he **handles the fire** inside.

- He notices the storm, but he doesn't let it stee.

- He feels the wave, but he doesn't get pulled under.

- He honors the emotion, but lets **clarity lead his response**.

This is the work: To stay calm. To stay clear. To stay **centered**—no matter what's happening outside or inside. That's masculine frame. That's **steel spine, calm heart** in motion.

Creating a Safe Inner World

Every man walks through the world with an internal atmosphere—an emotional climate that either supports him… or silently works against him. Some men live inside a mental war zone. Their self-talk is brutal. Their inner critic never sleeps. They walk through life feeling like they're never enough, always behind, always on edge. And no matter how strong they appear on the outside, their inner world is ruled by tension, fear, and quiet self-rejection.

Grounded masculinity begins when a man turns inward and builds a place he can trust. Not a fantasy. Not an ego shell. But a solid, steady, emotionally safe inner world—where he can feel without shame, think without spiraling, and be fully himself without judgment.

Here's how to start building that foundation.

1. Reclaim Your Inner Voice

Your inner world is shaped by the voice you speak to yourself with. For many men, that voice isn't even theirs—it's an echo of criticism from a parent, coach, teacher, or society.

Ask yourself:

- When I fail, what do I say to myself?

- When I'm alone, how do I treat myself?

- Do I speak to myself the way I'd speak to someone I respect?

If your inner dialogue is filled with sarcasm, shame, or self-contempt, your nervous system never gets a chance to rest. You live in constant emotional tension, even when no one is attacking you.

Rewrite the tone of your mind. You don't need fake positivity—you need honesty spoken with strength and self-respect.

Try this:

- Replace "I'm such an idiot" with "That wasn't my best move. Let's adjust."

- Replace "Nobody respects me" with "Where am I giving my power away?"

- Replace "I'm not good enough" with "I'm in progress, and I don't flinch."

Your inner voice sets the emotional climate you live in. Make it firm, not cruel. Clear, not crushing. Honest, not hostile.

2. Make Space for the Full Range of Emotion

Most men only feel safe in two emotional states: neutral or angry. Everything else—sadness, fear, tenderness, shame—is seen as weakness. So, they bottle it up. Bury it. Or act it out sideways in destructive ways. But buried emotion becomes background noise. It fogs your focus. It leaks into your tone, posture, and energy. Grounded men don't avoid emotion. They feel fully, process calmly, and express selectively. To create a safe inner world, you need to stop treating emotion like a threat.

Try this:

- Sit still when you feel discomfort. Don't distract. Breathe through it.

- Journal your emotion in one sentence: "Right now I feel ___ because ___."

- Let yourself cry, rage, or grieve in private without judgment. That's not weakness—it's emotional strength in motion.

A man who gives himself space to feel becomes emotionally bulletproof—not because he avoids emotion, but because he knows how to handle it.

◆ 3. Set Internal Boundaries

You wouldn't let someone else insult you, belittle you, or lie to you constantly. So why allow it from your own mind? A grounded man sets boundaries inside his head.

That means:

- Not indulging destructive thought loops

- Not letting shame hijack your identity

- Not giving airtime to outdated, limiting beliefs

When a toxic thought shows up, call it out:

"This story isn't true anymore."

"This fear is trying to protect me, but it's not leading me." "That's old programming. I choose a better thought now."

You become grounded by becoming a firm leader of your own mind.

◆ 4. Create Rituals That Restore Inner Peace

A safe inner world doesn't just happen. You build it with habits—rituals that reconnect you with clarity, strength, and presence.

These can include:

- Silent walks or morning stillness

- Breathwork or meditation (5–10 minutes a day)

- Grounding music or journaling by candlelight at night

- Solo time in nature—no phone, no noise

What matters isn't how the ritual looks, but what it gives you: A reset. A return to center. A reminder that your peace doesn't come from control—it comes from internal alignment.

◆ 5. Lead Yourself Like a Brother, Not a Bully

The final step in creating a safe inner world is to become your own ally.

Imagine if you spoke to yourself like a seasoned older brother:

- Firm, but never cruel.

- Honest, but never shaming.

- Holding you accountable, but always on your side.

When you lead yourself with grounded compassion—not weakness, but real understanding—you stop living in fear of your flaws. You start moving through life with quiet self-trust. And others feel it.

Because the man who is safe inside himself... Doesn't chase. Doesn't panic. Doesn't collapse when tested. He stands firm, not because the world is stable— But because he is.

Final Thoughts: The Inner World Creates the Outer Frame

Masculine frame is built inside-out. A man who creates a safe inner world becomes the kind of man people feel safe around. He doesn't perform. He doesn't posture. He doesn't need noise to prove his power. Because he's at home in himself and that—more than anything—is what makes him unshakable.

13

The Calm Within the Storm - Stoicism

Emotional Resilience as a Superpower

S trength without emotional control is just noise. Intellect without emotional resilience is just potential. A man can be physically dominant, financially successful, or intellectually brilliant— but if his emotions rule him, **he's still not in command**.

True power is not the absence of emotion. It's the ability to *feel fully* without being *ruled blindly*. This is emotional resilience: the **superpower that separates grounded men from reactive men**. It's not flashy, but it's rare. And in a chaotic world, it's magnetic.

◆ The World Doesn't Reward Outbursts

Modern life constantly tempts you to overreact—through conflict, rejection, stress, embarrassment, and uncertainty. And many men take the bait. They rage when they're disrespected. Collapse when they're misunderstood. Withdraw when things don't go their way.

They live like leaves in the wind—pulled in every direction by emotion. But **emotional reactivity leaks power**. It says to the world:

"I don't govern myself—my environment does."

Emotional resilience is the opposite. It says:

"I feel everything, but I choose my response."

That is frame. That is leadership. That is masculinity under control.

◆ What Emotional Resilience Actually Looks Like

It's not being robotic or cold. It's being fully human—but **centered**. Here's what it looks like in real time:

- You stay steady when someone insults you, because your worth isn't on trial.

- You keep breathing when the pressure mounts, because stress doesn't own your response.

- You feel sadness, disappointment, or anger—and still move forward with clarity.

This is the man who listens during an argument without needing to dominate it. This is the leader who doesn't fold under chaos but becomes sharper because of it. This is the father, brother, partner, and friend who **people trust** with their vulnerability—because he can handle his own.

◆ Why Most Men Aren't Emotionally Resilient

Because no one taught them how to be. They were told to suppress emotion. Or express it with force. They were never taught to observe it, regulate it, or lead with it. So most men walk around **emotionally fragile**—masking it with bravado, withdrawal, or passive aggression. Emotional resilience is not instinctual—it's a skill. And it can be trained, like strength.

◆ How to Build It Daily

1. Regulate Before Reacting

The first move of a resilient man is simple: **pause**. When emotion surges—breathe first, speak second. Give your nervous system 10 seconds to stabilize. You'll gain 10x the clarity.

2. Separate Feeling from Identity

You can feel anger without *being* angry. You can feel fear without *being* fearful. Resilient men create space between the emotion and their sense of self. That space is where strength lives.

3. Reframe Adversity as Training

Stress doesn't break a resilient man—it **refines** him. Every challenge becomes a rep for your emotional strength.

Ask: "What is this moment building in me?"

4. Reflect, Don't Ruminate

After emotional events, don't bury them—**process** them. Journaling, silent walks, or conscious reflection allow you to extract lessons instead of wounds.

5. Return to Center, Again and Again

Even the strongest men lose their calm sometimes. But resilient men **return quickly**. They don't spiral. They reset. That bounce-back speed is what separates grounded men from emotionally reactive boys.

Final Thoughts: Calm Is Your Competitive Edge

In a world that rewards loudness, **calm is a quiet revolution**. While others react—you respond. While others fall apart—you remain composed. While others panic—you lead.

Emotional resilience doesn't make you untouchable. It makes you **unshakable**. It's not about suppression—it's about ownership. It's not about avoidance—it's about clarity under pressure. It's not about being perfect—it's about becoming **so grounded in yourself that nothing outside of you dictates who you are**. Steel spine. Calm heart. Unbreakable presence.

That's emotional resilience. That's masculine power. That's your superpower.

Daily Stoic Practices

Steel is forged in fire. Stoic strength is forged in repetition. You don't become stoic by reading philosophy. You become stoic by **living deliberately**—by showing up to life each day with a calm mind, a strong spine, and clear standards.

Stoicism isn't about being emotionally flat or detached. It's about training your nervous system, your thoughts, and your behavior to **stay grounded in clarity**, no matter what life throws at you. The practices below are simple. But don't mistake simple for easy. These rituals, done daily, are how you build the core of a man who doesn't flinch under pressure.

◆ 1. Morning Framing – Own the Day Before It Owns You

Stoics don't stumble into their day. They **pre-frame** it. They mentally rehearse what may happen and commit to **how they will respond**. Start each morning with this 5-minute frame:

Ask yourself:

- *What is likely to challenge me today?*

- *What mood or trigger could knock me off center?*

- *What kind of man do I choose to be regardless of what happens?*

Then anchor the day with this affirmation:

"I am not here to be controlled by events. I am here to meet them with strength, calm, and clarity." **This is your first act of leadership—over yourself.**

◆ 2. Moment of Mastery – Pause, Then Proceed

Throughout the day, life will test you:

The rude email. The impatient partner. The unexpected failure. Most people react automatically. Stoic men **insert a pause**.

Practice the "sacred second":

- When triggered—breathe.

- When insulted—observe.

- When uncertain—slow down.

This isn't weakness. It's power under control. Each pause becomes a rep for emotional strength. Over time, your nervous system learns:

"We don't flinch. We don't rush. We respond with purpose."

◆ 3. Negative Visualization – Train the Mind for Reality

One of the most misunderstood Stoic tools is **premeditatio malorum**— "premeditation of evils." It's not pessimism. It's preparation.

Once a day, briefly imagine:

- A key plan failing.

- A person disappointing you.

- A goal being delayed.

Then ask:

"If this happens, how will I remain grounded?"

"What do I still control?"

This rewires your mind to stop fearing loss and start trusting your inner stability. It shrinks fear. It builds readiness. It makes you anti-fragile.

◆ 4. Evening Review – The Stoic Debrief

Your growth isn't in your wins. It's in your **reflection**. Each night, spend 5 minutes in silence or journaling. Ask:

- *Where did I keep my frame today?*

- *Where did I let emotion or ego take the wheel?*

- *What can I do better tomorrow—with no shame, just ownership?*

This creates self-accountability without self-punishment. It's how you go from theory to transformation. **Growth without ego. Correction without collapse. This is how you sharpen your edge daily.**

◆ 5. Voluntary Discomfort – Build Strength by Choice

The Stoics knew comfort makes men soft. So they trained themselves to stay calm in controlled adversity.

Choose one small hardship daily:

- Cold shower

- Intense workout

- Fasting for a few hours

- Silence in a moment of anger

- Speaking your truth when it's uncomfortable

Why? Because every time you choose discomfort, you teach your body:

"We can handle this."

You make adversity familiar, and you make yourself harder to disturb.

Final Thoughts: Discipline is Peace

Stoicism isn't something you turn on when life gets hard. It's a **way of being**—built through daily actions. You don't need to be perfect. You need to be **consistent**.

The calm man isn't lucky. He's trained. He's rehearsed peace in the small moments so he can stand tall in the storm.

- Your frame is shaped in the morning.

- Your power is tested in the pause.

- Your character is revealed at night.

- Your edge is sharpened through discomfort.

Do this daily—not to impress anyone, but to become the kind of man **you yourself can respect**. Steel spine. Calm heart. Stoic mind. Day by day. Practice by practice. Storm by storm.

Responding, not Reacting

"Between stimulus and response, there is a space. In that space is our power to choose our response." – Viktor Frankl Life is full of triggers. People will test you. Situations will blindside you. Emotions will rise.

But the man who is reactive gives his power away—to emotion, to circumstance, to the approval or disapproval of others. The man who responds, on the other hand, remains the author of his behavior. He is no longer a puppet of impulse. He becomes a **creator of outcomes**.

This is not just self-control. It is **self-command**—and it sits at the very core of masculine frame.

◆ **The Cost of Reactivity**

Reactivity is fast, emotional, and unconscious. It feels satisfying in the moment—snapping back, storming out, over-explaining—but it **fractures your influence** and weakens your presence.

Reactivity:

- Makes you easy to manipulate.

- Signals emotional immaturity.

- Breaks trust, especially in leadership or relationships.

- Leaves you with regret and cleanup.

A reactive man may win arguments. But he **loses respect**—from others and from himself.

◆ **Response Is a Choice, Not a Delay**

Responding doesn't mean you're passive or indifferent. It means you've **matured beyond the need to act from the first emotion** that shows up.

To respond means to:

- Pause.

- Assess.

- Choose.

You still take action. You still stand your ground. But you do it from **alignment**, not from emotional chaos. This is where masculine presence is built—not in suppression, but in intentional restraint.

◆ **The 3-Second Rule of Stoic Men**

When tension hits—when you're triggered, provoked, or emotionally stirred—use the internal **3-second rule**:

1. **Breathe.** One deep breath. In through the nose, out through the mouth.

2. **Observe.** What emotion is rising? What story is playing in your mind?

3. **Choose.** Ask: *"What response aligns with who I am and what I stand for?"*

In those three seconds, you take back control. You move from being at the mercy of the moment to **mastering the moment**.

◆ Leading with Stillness

When you respond instead of react, you create space—not just for yourself, but for others. You set the tone. You bring clarity to chaos. You lead through grounded energy.

This stillness:

- Commands respect in conversation.

- Disarms escalation.

- Signals emotional strength.

- Builds trust—fast.

In personal and professional life, people instinctively follow the man who **isn't thrown off course** by pressure. Who can take a hit—verbal, emotional, situational—and still choose his direction. That's not weakness. That's **high-level strength**.

◆ Practice: Build the Response Muscle

Responding is a discipline. Start training it with these micro-reps:

- Next time someone interrupts you, pause before replying.

- When criticized, resist the urge to defend—ask, "What's the useful piece here?"

- In a disagreement, lower your voice instead of raising it.

- When anxiety hits, sit with the feeling instead of escaping it.

These small moves stack over time. Each one rewires your brain and body for **deliberate, composed action**.

Final Thoughts: The Calm Edge

In a reactive world, the man who can stay composed becomes rare—and magnetic. He isn't just harder to provoke. He's harder to ignore.

He speaks less but says more. He moves less but influences more.

He fights less, but wins more—because he's not ruled by impulse, but by principle. So when the moment heats up, remember this:

Don't just do something.

Stand still, breathe, and then move with intent.

That is how grounded men lead. That is how masculine frame holds. That is how **steel spine, calm heart** becomes reality.

The Discipline of Control

"He who controls others may be powerful, but he who has mastered himself is mightier still." – Lao Tzu

Control is often misunderstood. It's not about dominating the external world or forcing outcomes. It's about mastering the internal—your emotions, your reactions, your thoughts. The only true control you have is over yourself.

The discipline of control is the bedrock of masculine frame. It's the quiet, relentless work of becoming the man who chooses his actions over his impulses, his direction over his circumstances, and his inner peace over external chaos.

◆ External Control Is a Myth

In a world that constantly demands more, faster, and better, many men believe control is something they can force. They attempt to control their environment—people, outcomes, situations. But the reality is, you cannot control the external world, no matter how hard you try.

What you can control, and what you must focus on, is how you respond to the world around you.

The more you attempt to grip life tightly, the more it slips through your fingers. You can't control what others say, how they behave, or even most of the circumstances you face. But you can control your reaction to them. The discipline of control is about recognizing where your true power lies—and that is within you.

◆ Self-Control as the Gateway to Freedom

Mastery of self isn't about repression or suppression. It's about freedom—freedom to act in alignment with your values, your goals, and your higher purpose, even when everything around you is trying to knock you off course.

Self-control gives you the freedom to:

- Stay calm in moments of stress.

- Lead with clarity when others are confused.

- Make decisions based on reason, not impulse.

- Hold your ground when emotions threaten to cloud your judgment.

Self-control isn't restrictive—it's empowering. The Stoics knew this well: they embraced the discipline of control because it liberated them from external chaos, leaving them to focus on what truly mattered—their own character and growth.

- **The Three Pillars of Control**

1. **Emotional Control:**

   Your emotions are powerful, but you are more powerful. Emotional control means you can experience anger, frustration, sadness, or joy—but you don't let those emotions dictate your actions. The goal is not to eliminate feelings, but to direct them. When you control your emotional state, you can choose how to engage with life, not just react to it.

2. **Mental Control:**

   Your thoughts are like water—they flow in and out constantly, sometimes turbulent, sometimes calm. Mental control means you don't let your thoughts run wild, especially when they're unhelpful or negative. It means choosing your focus—deciding where to direct your energy and attention. When you control your mind, you direct your focus toward the things that serve you, not the distractions that drain you.

3. **Behavioral Control:**

   Your actions are the result of your thoughts and emotions, but ultimately, you control them. This is where your character is forged. Every day, you choose how to show up in the world—whether you respond with grace in a heated moment, whether you stand firm in your values, or whether you give in to temptation or laziness. Behavioral control is the backbone of masculinity—it's where your values meet your actions.

- **How to Develop the Discipline of Control**

1. **Start Small: Build the Muscle**

   Control isn't a switch you can flip—it's a muscle that you must exercise daily. Start small. The next time you feel a trigger, pause for just three seconds. Breathe, assess, and choose your response. Slowly, you'll build the habit of self-control, and it will extend to every part of your life.

2. Create Boundaries

Mastery over yourself begins with boundaries—personal lines you don't cross, no matter what. Whether it's limiting your reactions to stress, saying "no" when necessary, or protecting your energy by avoiding toxic influences, boundaries are your first defense against external pressure.

3. Embrace Delayed Gratification

The ability to delay gratification is one of the clearest markers of self-discipline. Every time you choose the long-term reward over the short-term satisfaction, you strengthen your capacity for self-control. This is why Stoic practices like voluntary discomfort—whether fasting, cold showers, or challenging workouts—are powerful. They train you to say no to your impulses and build your resilience.

4. Own Your Triggers

Triggers are not inherently bad. They are simply signals that point to where you're not in control. Identify your triggers—be it anger, insecurity, jealousy, or frustration—and work to desensitize yourself to them. The next time they appear, use it as an opportunity to pause, reflect, and recalibrate your response.

5. Practice Self-Reflection

Self-control thrives on self-awareness. At the end of each day, take a moment to reflect:

o   Where did you stay in control?

o   Where did you lose control?

o   What could you have done differently?

Reflection makes self-control a conscious practice, not just a reaction. It allows you to fine-tune your responses and improve day by day.

Final Thoughts: Control is the Ultimate Freedom

True strength comes not from dominating the world around you, but from dominating your inner world. It's not the loud man who commands attention—it's the one who has the discipline to remain composed. It's not the man who forces things—it's the one who has the control to let things unfold in their own time.

The discipline of control is the true measure of masculine power. Master yourself, and you master your life. Steel spine. Calm heart. Control within. This is the disciplined man. This is the man who shapes his world with quiet power.

14

High Vibration Masculinity

What 'High Vibration' Really Means (Beyond New Age)

When most people hear the term **"high vibration"**, their minds might immediately jump to the world of **new age spirituality** or mysticism. Words like "energy," "aura," or "frequency" might trigger images of crystal healing, meditation retreats, or the latest self-help fad.

But let's clear the air here: **high vibration masculinity** isn't about mystical energy or abstract ideals. It's about **living at your highest potential**, the version of yourself that is aligned with strength, purpose, and integrity. High vibration masculinity is rooted in something tangible—a grounded presence, emotional mastery, and the unwavering belief in **your ability to influence the world through your actions**.

◆ What High Vibration Really Means

At its core, high vibration refers to the **quality of energy** you emit, and how that energy impacts both your internal world and the world around you. It's the combination of your emotional, mental, and physical states that create a **positive force** in the world.

High vibration masculinity goes far beyond simply being "positive" or "energetic." It is about being **authentic** and **intentional** with your energy. It is about being in tune with your **purpose** and aligning your thoughts, actions, and emotions to support that purpose, no matter the external circumstances.

In the world of high vibration masculinity, this energy manifests in a powerful **balance** between inner peace and outward strength. It's about **exerting**

influence, not through force or dominance, but through **the clarity and confidence** that emanates from your every word, move, and interaction.

◆ The Practical Application of High Vibration

While the term may seem abstract or disconnected from everyday life, high vibration masculinity has very real applications. It's the foundation of powerful leadership, emotional intelligence, and personal magnetism. Here's how it works in practice:

1. **Authenticity Over "Good Vibes"**

   High vibration doesn't mean wearing a constant smile or trying to force positivity into every situation. It's about being **authentic—** showing up as your true self, even when it's uncomfortable. This means embracing your flaws, your strengths, and everything that makes you unique. **Your authentic energy is the highest vibration you can emit**—people feel it when you are fully in alignment with who you are.

2. **Emotional Mastery Over Emotional Reactivity**

   A high vibration man is not someone who is constantly bouncing between extremes of emotional highs and lows. He has mastered his emotions—not by suppressing them but by **choosing how to respond**. He understands that **true power lies in choosing his reactions**. By staying grounded in his emotional center, he radiates a calm yet dynamic presence that attracts respect and trust.

3. **Purpose-Driven Action Over Ego-Driven Reactivity**

   High vibration masculinity is **purpose-driven**. This means you aren't moving through life driven by ego or the need for approval; you act with clarity, alignment, and intention. When you live with purpose, every action you take carries a certain energy—a **focused vibration** that's magnetic to others. People feel drawn to you because they can sense the clarity and direction you carry, without you having to say a word.

4. **Resilience and Inner Peace Over Chaos and Conflict**

One of the most powerful aspects of high vibration masculinity is the **ability to stay grounded in the midst of chaos**. This isn't about being emotionless or detached. Instead, it's about **having the internal resilience** to face challenges with composure and confidence. High vibration men are not rattled easily—they respond with **calm authority** instead of reactionary force. This inner peace radiates out, creating an environment of stability for everyone around them.

◆ **Why High Vibration Masculinity Is Not Just a Buzzword**

In the same way that **leadership** or **influence** are often misunderstood, so too is high vibration masculinity. It's not about following trends or spiritual clichés—it's about **embodying the highest version of yourself** and operating from a place of deep personal integrity.

This energy isn't something you can fake or force. It requires constant self-awareness and an **ongoing commitment to growth**. It's about choosing **quality over quantity** in your thoughts, actions, and interactions. When you begin to operate from this higher frequency, **everything shifts**: you'll find that you attract better opportunities, more meaningful relationships, and respect—without even trying.

In practical terms, high vibration masculinity means:

*   **Owning your choices**, knowing that your decisions are a reflection of your core values and beliefs.

*   **Being emotionally intelligent**—able to express vulnerability and strength in equal measure.

*   **Embodying physical vitality**, whether that means being in peak physical shape, engaging in regular exercise, or simply having a level of energy that reflects your internal power.

*   **Constantly evolving**, with a focus on becoming the best version of yourself, not for external validation, but because it aligns with your personal growth.

◆ **High Vibration as a Reflection of Inner Mastery**

Here's the bottom line: **high vibration masculinity is not about being 'extra' or adopting superficial habits**. It's about **mastering your inner world**. It's the ability to be **so grounded, so clear, and so purposeful** that your energy flows effortlessly into the world, influencing those around you in ways you might not even realize.

By aligning your thoughts, emotions, and actions with your true self, you naturally raise your vibration. This is not some magical "new age" concept; it's simply the **result of a life lived with purpose**, intention, and integrity. High vibration masculinity means you are **fully in tune with your authentic power**, radiating confidence, resilience, and grace.

This is the **real power** of high vibration masculinity: It's not about what you do, or how you look, or even how you talk—it's the **energy you emit** from being fully aligned with who you truly are.

Final Thoughts: Master the Inner, Master the Outer

High vibration masculinity is about being the man who **has mastered his inner self**. The more you raise your internal energy through authenticity, emotional mastery, and purpose, the more you become **magnetic to those around you**.

This isn't just about feeling "good" or being "positive"—it's about living with deep integrity, focus, and strength that leaves a lasting impression on everyone you meet. And in that, you have the power to not only transform yourself but to transform the world around you.

Raising Your Energetic Signature Through Integrity

Your **energetic signature** is the unique vibration that you radiate into the world, the invisible aura of energy that others pick up on before you even speak.

It's the combination of your thoughts, emotions, actions, and values, all converging into a distinct and powerful **personal frequency**.

What most people don't realize is that the most **powerful tool** you have for raising your energetic signature—the tool that will elevate your presence, influence, and impact—is something incredibly simple, yet profoundly transformative: **Integrity**.

When you live in alignment with your values, when your actions match your words, and when you embody the highest principles of authenticity and self-respect, you not only raise your own energy but also elevate the energy of those around you.

This is because **integrity** is one of the highest vibrational states a person can achieve. It creates clarity, trust, and a grounded sense of purpose. People are drawn to those who **embody their principles** because there's no discord in their energy—what they say, what they do, and who they are all align seamlessly.

◆ What is Integrity, Really?

Integrity isn't just about being "honest" or "doing the right thing." It's much deeper than that. **Integrity** is about **internal coherence**—the alignment between what you believe, how you think, and what you do. It's the absence of internal conflict. When you live with integrity, you are not torn between your values and your actions. They are one.

This coherence forms the foundation of your **energetic signature**. It's the authenticity of your being. People feel it the moment you enter a room; they sense your sincerity, your authenticity, and your power. There's an undeniable **magnetism** to someone who lives with integrity because it speaks to a deep trustworthiness and a **calm confidence** that only comes from being completely **aligned with one's true self**.

When you lack integrity, when there's a misalignment between your inner beliefs and your outward actions, your energetic signature feels disjointed. People may feel your **inauthenticity** or sense that you are **hiding something**, and as a result, they are less likely to trust or respect you.

217

How Integrity Raises Your Energetic Signature

1. ### Consistency of Action and Thought

   Integrity means you are the same person in every situation—there's no gap between who you are in private and who you are in public. This **consistency** creates a **powerful energetic frequency** because others know what to expect from you. They trust that you will follow through, and that trust becomes part of your **vibration**. It's no longer just your words that people listen to—it's the certainty in your actions and the reliability of your presence.

2. ### Deep Self-Respect

   Living with integrity means you respect your own values, boundaries, and truth. This self-respect is the **foundation** of your personal power. When you respect yourself in every decision, you naturally raise your **vibration** because you no longer have to worry about internal contradictions or self-doubt. People can feel that self-respect in the way you hold yourself, in the way you **carry your energy**, and in the way you interact with others. It emanates from you like a subtle force field, creating an invisible **aura of confidence** that draws others in.

3. ### Authentic Confidence

   Integrity creates the bedrock for **authentic confidence**. You no longer need to **prove** yourself to others because your energy is already aligned with your truth. This eliminates the need for external validation and shifts your focus toward **internal alignment**. Confident people don't boast—they simply **are**. Their energy speaks volumes because it's rooted in a **strong internal foundation**, not in the **desperate need for approval** or validation. This self-assurance becomes an attractive energy, inviting others to believe in you as much as you believe in yourself.

4. ### Clarity and Purpose

   When you live with integrity, your purpose becomes clearer. You understand who you are, what you stand for, and why you do what you do. This clarity is the **core of your energetic signature**. It allows you to move through life with direction, meaning, and intent. When you walk with a purpose, you become a **magnet for opportunities** because others are drawn to that sense of alignment. It is not just what you say that influences them—it's the **certainty** with which you speak it, and the **vibrational power** behind your words.

◆ The Practical Application of Integrity to Raise Your Energy

Raising your energetic signature through integrity doesn't just happen overnight—it's a **deliberate practice**. Here are some steps you can take to begin living with greater integrity and, in turn, raise your energetic signature:

1. Live in Alignment with Your Values

The first step is to identify what you truly value—your core principles. Whether it's honesty, respect, loyalty, or any other value, living in alignment with them creates a seamless flow of energy. When your decisions are based on your **true values**, your energy becomes **coherent and powerful**.

2. Follow Through on Your Commitments

When you give your word, keep it. This simple act of **commitment and follow-through** builds **trust**, which is the foundation of integrity. Over time, people will sense the **reliability** in your energy, and this trust will compound, raising your energetic signature.

3. Practice Radical Honesty

Integrity is built on **honesty**—not just with others, but with yourself. Ask yourself the hard questions: Are you living according to your true self, or are you hiding parts of who you are to gain approval? Honesty with yourself will naturally **raise your vibration**, as it eliminates the inner turmoil and conflict that comes from living a divided life.

4. Set Boundaries Based on Self-Respect

Boundaries are a crucial part of integrity. To maintain your high-vibration energy, you must be willing to set and enforce boundaries that protect your **energy**. When you set clear boundaries based on self-respect, you automatically

elevate your vibration by refusing to tolerate any behavior or influence that compromises your values.

5. Forgive Yourself and Others

Holding on to guilt or resentment lowers your energetic frequency. Part of living with integrity is **making peace** with your past mistakes and forgiving others for their wrongs. This act of emotional release allows you to **move forward with a higher, more expansive energy**.

◆ The Long-Term Impact of Integrity on Your Energy

Living with integrity doesn't just raise your energetic signature—it **compounds over time**, growing stronger as you continue to practice it. Over weeks, months, and years, your energy will become more **magnetic**, your influence more profound, and your presence more **grounded**. The consistency with which you align your actions with your values will naturally elevate your vibration to a point where others are drawn to you, not because of what you do, but because of the **authentic power you exude**.

As you continue to raise your energetic signature through integrity, you will notice that you start attracting higher-level opportunities, deeper connections, and greater respect. This is because your energy no longer aligns with **fear or insecurity**—it aligns with your **highest self**. And when you live from that place, the world around you **responds** in kind.

Final Thoughts: Integrity as the Key to Lasting Power

In the end, high-vibration masculinity is not about flashy appearances or fleeting moments of success. It's about creating a **deep, unshakable power** rooted in integrity. When you raise your energetic signature by living in alignment with your truth, you not only change the energy within you—you **change the energy of the world around you**.

And that, in turn, makes you an irresistible force—one that influences and shapes the lives of others without ever needing to force or control them.

When your energy is pure, grounded, and consistent, you become a beacon of **authentic power** that is felt long after you leave the room. That is the true essence of high vibration masculinity.

Emotional Clarity and Self-Worth

One of the most powerful forces that shapes your energetic signature is the clarity with which you **understand and manage your emotions**. Emotional clarity is not just about feeling good or staying positive—it's about **having a clear, honest understanding of your emotional landscape** and acting from a place of **self-awareness**. When combined with **self-worth**, emotional clarity becomes the cornerstone of high vibration masculinity.

At the core of emotional clarity is the ability to **process emotions with awareness** rather than reacting to them impulsively. It's the ability to feel deeply without being overwhelmed, to acknowledge your feelings without letting them control you. This is where **self-worth** comes in—because when you value yourself deeply, you allow yourself the space to feel and express emotions without guilt or shame.

Together, **emotional clarity** and **self-worth** create an internal foundation that allows you to respond to life's challenges with **grace, strength, and resilience**. This combination not only elevates your emotional intelligence but also **raises your vibration**—you are no longer at the mercy of external circumstances; you are **anchored in your own power**, regardless of what's happening around you.

♦ **The Link Between Emotional Clarity and High Vibration Masculinity**

1. **Emotions as Messengers, Not Masters**

   High-vibration masculinity isn't about suppressing emotions or denying their presence; it's about **understanding** them and using them to your advantage. Emotions are not inherently good or bad—they are simply signals, messengers that offer valuable insight into your inner world. When you can process your emotions with clarity, you no longer allow them to dictate your behavior. Instead, you respond to them consciously. This emotional self-mastery **elevates your presence** because people sense your emotional control. They see someone who is not rattled by challenges but moves through them with intentional calmness and confidence.

2. **Embracing Vulnerability Without Weakness**

Vulnerability is often seen as a weakness, especially in a world that prizes stoic strength. However, high-vibration masculinity understands that true strength lies in the **willingness to be vulnerable**. Emotional clarity enables you to embrace vulnerability not as an admission of weakness, but as a powerful **act of self-trust and authenticity**. When you are clear on your emotions and self-worth, you can share your feelings, fears, and desires without losing your composure. This vulnerability is not a weakness; it's a profound **demonstration of emotional strength** that others will respect and be drawn to.

3. **Responding from a Place of Centered Power**

Emotional clarity and self-worth allow you to **respond, rather than react** to life's challenges. Instead of letting emotions like fear, anger, or frustration dictate your behavior, you are able to choose your responses from a place of inner calm. This is the essence of **emotional intelligence**—and it is one of the hallmarks of high-vibration masculinity. When you have a clear understanding of your emotions and **deep confidence in your worth**, your reactions become **grounded in wisdom**, not driven by impulse. This not only prevents unnecessary conflict, but it also enhances your **influence** over situations, as people trust you to remain calm and decisive under pressure.

◆ **Building Emotional Clarity and Self-Worth**

1. **Reflect and Understand Your Emotions**

The first step in cultivating emotional clarity is to **acknowledge your emotions** without judgment. Ask yourself questions like, "Why am I feeling this way?" or "What is this emotion trying to teach me?" Take

222

time to journal or meditate, allowing space for deep self-reflection. The more you understand your emotions, the clearer you become about how they influence your actions. With emotional clarity, you are empowered to make choices based on your true feelings, rather than being swept away by **emotional turbulence**.

2. **Build Self-Worth Through Action and Integrity**

Self-worth doesn't come from external validation or achievements—it comes from **internal alignment**. The more you act in accordance with your values, the stronger your sense of self-worth becomes. Practice **self-respect** by honoring your commitments, speaking your truth, and holding yourself to a standard of integrity. **Self-worth grows when you consistently prove to yourself that you are worthy of respect**—both from others and from within. It's about **doing what's right, even when it's hard**. This builds an unshakable sense of self-belief, which becomes the foundation of your emotional clarity.

3. **Accept and Release Negative Emotions**

High-vibration masculinity isn't about avoiding or suppressing negative emotions—it's about **accepting them without fear**. When you experience emotions like anger, fear, or sadness, don't try to push them away. Instead, allow yourself to fully experience them, understand where they come from, and then let them pass through you. This practice of **non-attachment** to negative emotions allows you to retain emotional clarity, because you are not defined by what you feel in any given moment. You are able to observe your emotions objectively, without letting them cloud your judgment or derail your actions.

4. **Cultivate Positive Self-Talk**

Self-worth is deeply connected to the way you speak to yourself. Your inner dialogue has the power to either **build you up or tear you down**. Practice speaking to yourself with compassion, respect, and encouragement. **Affirmations**, mindfulness, and positive self-talk are all tools that help rewire your subconscious and reinforce your **sense of self-worth**. The more you believe in your own value, the stronger your emotional clarity will become, because you won't feel the need to prove yourself to others. **Your self-belief is rooted in your own recognition of your inherent value**.

◆ The Power of Emotional Clarity and Self-Worth in High-Vibration Masculinity

When you combine emotional clarity with self-worth, you become a man who is **centered, resilient, and magnetic**. People are drawn to your grounded energy because they feel safe in your presence—**your emotional steadiness is a reflection of your inner strength**. You don't need to shout for attention, because your energy speaks louder than words.

As your emotional clarity deepens, so does your ability to lead with purpose, influence with authenticity, and connect with others on a meaningful level. **Self-worth** will no longer be something you seek externally; it will radiate from within, naturally elevating your vibration and attracting the right people, opportunities, and experiences.

When you are emotionally clear and anchored in your self-worth, you create an energy that **flows freely**, unburdened by doubt, fear, or insecurity. Your **high-vibration masculinity** is no longer dependent on external validation, because you are confident in who you are and how you show up in the world.

In essence, emotional clarity and self-worth don't just make you resilient—they make you **irresistibly magnetic**, allowing you to inspire others and lead with power, confidence, and grace.

Becoming a Beacon for Others

One of the most profound effects of cultivating high-vibration masculinity is the impact you have on the world around you. As you raise your energetic frequency through practices like emotional clarity, self-worth, and integrity, something incredible begins to happen: you become a beacon for others. People are naturally drawn to you—not because of flashy words or attention-seeking behavior, but because of the authenticity and depth that radiate from within.

The energy you emit has the power to influence, uplift, and inspire those around you. In a world full of noise, uncertainty, and chaos, you become the calm in the storm, the steady anchor that others instinctively gravitate toward. Your high-vibration masculinity is not about ego or dominance, but about leading by example—embodying values that inspire others to step into their own strength and authenticity.

◆ The Power of Leading by Example

People are not only influenced by what you say—they are profoundly impacted by how you live. When your actions, thoughts, and energy are aligned, you become the embodiment of the qualities you want to inspire in others. This kind of authentic leadership doesn't require forceful action or manipulation; instead, it draws others in naturally.

Your life becomes a living example of what's possible when someone operates at their highest potential. It's through actions that people begin to see the depth of your character—your commitment to your values, your ability to stay grounded under pressure, your willingness to speak your truth, and your unwavering consistency. People see this and are inspired to adopt those same principles in their own lives.

For example, when you show up consistently with integrity, others notice. When you act with self-respect, maintain emotional clarity, and lead by example, people feel your genuine power and will look to you as a source of inspiration. Your energy becomes contagious, and in turn, others start to reflect that same energy in their lives.

◆ How High-Vibration Masculinity Impacts Others

1. Lifting Others with Your Presence

You don't need to speak loudly or perform grand gestures to lift others up. The energy you project simply by being yourself can elevate a room. High-vibration masculinity is about presence—the quiet strength that emanates from within. When you walk into a room, others feel your groundedness, your calm, and your certainty. People gravitate toward you, not because you seek attention, but because your energy is steady, powerful, and safe. They feel seen, heard, and uplifted by your presence.

2. Inspiring Growth Through Example

True leaders are not those who force others to follow them—they are the ones who inspire others to grow and evolve. As you embody high-vibration masculinity, you naturally encourage the same in others. People around you will start to rise to the occasion, often without you needing to say a word. Your example shows them what is possible: personal growth, self-mastery, emotional control, and a life of integrity. They look at you and think, "If he can do it, so can I." This is how high-vibration masculinity becomes a beacon for others—through the transformative power of example.

3. Creating Safe Spaces for Others

A key aspect of becoming a beacon for others is creating an environment where they feel safe to be themselves—free from judgment or pressure. As you cultivate emotional clarity, self-worth, and integrity, you naturally build trust with those around you. People feel comfortable being vulnerable in your presence because they see that you do not demand perfection from them, but instead encourage growth and authenticity. Your inner strength and emotional stability create a safe space for others to explore their own vulnerabilities, express their emotions, and find clarity.

◆ Practical Ways to Become a Beacon for Others

1. Be Consistent in Your Actions and Words

Consistency is the hallmark of someone who lives in integrity. When your actions align with your values, others begin to trust you. They know you will show up as you are—whether that's in a difficult situation or a celebratory one. Living consistently allows people to feel safe in your presence because they can count on you to be reliable and true to yourself. This consistency makes you an anchor for others, as they can always look to you for support, guidance, and strength.

2. **Lead with Compassion and Empathy**

High-vibration masculinity is not about suppressing emotions—it's about understanding and expressing them with grace and wisdom. When you lead with compassion and empathy, others are drawn to you because they see that you truly care about their well-being. Being emotionally available for others, listening deeply without judgment, and showing empathy during challenging times make you a source of comfort and guidance.

3. **Encourage and Elevate Those Around You**

High-vibration masculinity is contagious—it spreads through the energy you project. Take the time to encourage and uplift others. Celebrate their victories, help them navigate their challenges, and show them that they are worthy of success. When you invest in the growth of others, they begin to mirror that same behavior and rise to their potential. You become not just a beacon of power but also a catalyst for the growth of those around you.

4. **Stay True to Your Values, Even in Adversity**

In challenging situations, your values and principles are tested. When you stay committed to your integrity even in the face of pressure, people will look to you as a source of strength and guidance. They will see that your high-vibration masculinity is not contingent on circumstances—it is rooted in something deeper. This kind of unwavering strength encourages others to stand firm in their own beliefs, knowing that they, too, can navigate life with the same integrity and inner power.

◆ The Ripple Effect of Your High-Vibration Energy

The most powerful aspect of becoming a beacon for others is the ripple effect that your energy creates. As you embody high-vibration masculinity, you set off a chain reaction that influences those around you in ways you may not even see. Your calm, confident presence encourages others to be more grounded, your leadership empowers them to take action, and your empathy inspires them to open up and grow.

This ripple effect extends beyond just the people you interact with directly. As those you impact grow stronger and more empowered, they, in turn, become beacons for others. Your high-vibration masculinity sets in motion a cycle of growth that spreads exponentially—creating a world where more and more people are empowered to live at their highest potential.

Final Thoughts: The Ripple of Your Authentic Power

Becoming a beacon for others isn't about seeking attention or recognition—it's about living authentically and allowing your actions, your energy, and your presence to inspire others to become the best version of themselves. As you embody high-vibration masculinity, you naturally elevate those around you, helping them to rise in ways they never imagined.

The true power of high-vibration masculinity lies not in what you accomplish for yourself, but in how you impact the lives of others. You become a living example of what's possible when a man is grounded, clear, and confident in his own skin. Your authentic presence, self-mastery, and unwavering strength act as a beacon that guides others toward their own greatness.

Conclusion: Becoming the Frame

Integration of the Traits

As you reach the conclusion of this journey, it's important to understand that becoming the frame is not about mastering each trait in isolation. The true power of **masculine frame** lies in the **integration** of these individual components into one cohesive presence. The traits—each one powerful on its own—are meant to work together, creating a **harmonious energy** that influences the world around you in a profound and transformative way.

The traits of masculine frame—your **deep voice, stoicism, gravitas, charisma, authority, leadership, dominance, influence, silence, authenticity, groundedness, high vibration masculinity, and emotional resilience**—are not simply boxes to check. They are aspects of a **dynamic system** that, when integrated properly, create a man who is not only powerful in action but magnetic in presence.

♦ **The Holistic Approach to Mastery**

You have explored the importance of each trait individually, from the commanding tone of your voice to the quiet power of your silence. However, in practice, it is the **integration of these traits** that will give you a presence of undeniable strength. **True mastery comes when you blend the qualities in a way that feels natural to who you are**, so they become second nature in how you carry yourself, respond to situations, and lead others.

- **Deep Voice & Executive Presence:** A strong voice combined with executive presence creates not only a commanding presence but also an ability to influence and inspire confidence in others.

- **Charisma & Gravitas:** Charisma makes you magnetic, drawing people to you, while gravitas gives you the weight and substance to back up your magnetism. Together, they create a persona that attracts and leads, yet commands respect.

- **Stoicism & Leadership:** Your ability to remain stoic, calm, and unshaken under pressure strengthens your leadership abilities, allowing you to make clear decisions and guide others with authority and wisdom.

- **Dominance & Influence:** While dominance is about maintaining your space and asserting your will, influence is about **drawing others toward your vision** without coercion. The true integration of these traits allows you to dominate not through force, but through the natural pull of your presence and guidance.

◆ A Seamless Presence: From Trait to Being

When these traits are fully integrated, they are no longer a checklist of behaviors or tactics you need to manage. They become **part of your being**—a seamless expression of your **masculine essence**. You are no longer thinking about how to use your deep voice in certain situations, or remembering to stand tall and speak with authority. These traits flow naturally from you, **without effort**. They become the very fabric of your character, the foundation upon which your influence and respect are built.

This kind of integration requires patience and practice. It's about **creating harmony** between the mind, body, and spirit—so that you operate not just with strength but with **balance**. It's the balance between power and grace, silence and expression, action and contemplation. You can't force these traits into place; they need to be **earned** through real-life experiences, challenges, and growth. As you continue to practice these principles, they will begin to align within you, like pieces of a puzzle falling into place.

◆ Practical Steps for Integration

1. **Consistent Practice:** Mastery of masculine frame comes through consistent, daily practice. Focus on one trait at a time but aim to integrate the lessons across your day-to-day life. For example, when practicing stoicism, take the opportunity to also exercise emotional regulation and

groundedness. When focusing on influence, pay attention to how you combine that with silence and active listening. The integration process happens naturally when you **apply** each trait in tandem with the others.

2. **Self-Reflection:** Regular self-reflection is crucial to ensure that these traits are not merely superficial qualities but are deeply rooted in who you are. Ask yourself: **How do I respond to challenges?** Do I remain calm and in control? How can I bring more authenticity into my leadership? Journaling, meditation, and conversation with trusted mentors can help you **gauge your progress** and **identify areas for improvement**.

3. **Feedback from Others:** One of the most powerful ways to gauge your integration is by seeking feedback from those you trust. **Other people's perceptions** can offer you valuable insights into how you are living the traits of masculine frame. Ask how you come across in meetings, in social settings, and in times of stress. Are you embodying the qualities you want to project? Feedback allows you to refine your approach and get closer to embodying the full essence of masculine frame.

4. **Embodiment in Action:** Theory is useful, but embodiment is where true transformation occurs. Go out and **live with intention**. Practice asserting yourself with authority in situations that require it, listen with focused presence in conversations, and step into leadership roles that stretch you. The more you act from a place of integration, the more naturally these traits will become part of who you are.

◆ **A Life of Impact**

Ultimately, the goal of integrating these traits into your life is not only to **become the man you were always meant to be** but to have a **lasting impact on the world**. Masculine frame is about creating a **life of influence, respect, and presence**—and through the integration of these traits, you will leave a legacy of strength and leadership that can positively shape those around you.

When you live in full alignment with these traits, **you will naturally inspire others** to elevate themselves. Your calm strength will become a source of inspiration, your grounded leadership will create ripple effects of growth, and your authenticity will draw others to find their own true power. The frame you build becomes not only a force for your own success but a foundation for the success of others.

As you step forward, becoming a beacon of high-vibration masculinity, you will find that **the world starts to reflect back the energy you project**. People will respect you not just for what you do, but for who you are—because you are the embodiment of a life lived with purpose, power, and integrity.

In the end, becoming the frame is about embracing **your deepest essence** and integrating it into every aspect of your life. It is about becoming a man who is strong in his mind, body, and spirit—who lives with purpose, leads with authenticity, and commands influence through his presence. **This journey is yours**—and it is just beginning.

The Lifelong Journey of Mastery

Mastery is not a destination; it's a continuous, evolving journey. **Becoming the frame**—the embodiment of masculine strength, grounded power, and influence—requires ongoing commitment, introspection, and refinement. You will never reach a point where you can say, "I am fully there." Instead, you will constantly grow, adapt, and deepen your understanding of yourself and the world around you.

This is the beauty of **masculine frame**—it's a dynamic, ever-evolving force. Just as a mountain is constantly shaped by the elements, so too is your frame shaped by your experiences, challenges, triumphs, and failures. The journey of mastery is one of **endless self-discovery** and **continuous growth**, and it's this very pursuit that will keep you sharp, humble, and powerful.

◆ The Path of Continuous Self-Improvement

No matter how much you master today, there is always more to learn and refine tomorrow. **Mastery isn't static**—it's the willingness to keep growing, to keep facing new challenges, and to keep improving your understanding of yourself and the world around you.

Every day offers opportunities to grow in ways you may not expect. You may face new challenges that test your emotional resilience, your leadership skills, or your ability to stay grounded in chaos. But it's in these moments that the most profound lessons are learned. As you continue to evolve, you'll discover that mastery doesn't lie in perfection but in the **ongoing process of becoming**. This means accepting that you will stumble at times, face setbacks, and experience moments of doubt—but those are part of the journey. They are **not failures**; they are lessons that build your character and deepen your strength.

The key to **true mastery** is your **ability to stay committed to growth**—no matter what. It's not about achieving perfection, but about continuously **raising the bar** for yourself and moving forward with intention, discipline, and resilience. Each day is an opportunity to move closer to becoming the best version of yourself.

◆ Embracing Change and Adaptability

As you embark on this journey, understand that the world is constantly changing, and so are you. New challenges will arise, new circumstances will unfold, and you will encounter different people who will push you to evolve in unexpected ways. **Adaptability is essential to mastery**. The traits of masculine frame are not rigid; they need to be adaptable to the different environments and challenges you face.

For example, the leadership skills you develop in one area of your life may need to evolve as you take on new roles or responsibilities. The way you express **gravitas** or **dominance** may shift depending on the context, but your underlying principles—emotional control, authenticity, and grounded power—should remain consistent. The journey of mastery is about understanding when to **lean into** certain traits and when to **hold back** or adjust your approach.

Adaptability allows you to **stay relevant,** to lead effectively in various situations, and to maintain your strength without becoming rigid. It keeps you from growing complacent or becoming stuck in old patterns, ensuring that your journey remains a **vibrant and ever-evolving process**.

◆ The Importance of Patience and Perseverance

Mastery isn't something that happens overnight. It requires **patience, perseverance,** and an unwavering commitment to the long road ahead. This journey of becoming the frame is not about quick fixes or shortcuts. It's about steady, consistent effort over time. You will experience moments of frustration, times when progress feels slow or non-existent. Yet, it is precisely in these moments that you will **build the most strength**.

Patience in the process is crucial. **Trust that each step forward**—no matter how small—matters. Even on the days when you don't feel like you're moving forward, you are. Every time you choose **discipline over distraction, calm over chaos,** and **integrity over convenience,** you are laying the foundation for a life of mastery.

Mastery is a journey that doesn't have a finish line. There will always be new frontiers to explore, deeper layers of understanding to uncover, and higher levels of achievement to strive for. **The key is to enjoy the journey itself,** understanding that the person you become along the way is just as important as what you accomplish.

◆ Realizing the Ripple Effect

As you continue on your journey, one of the most powerful aspects of mastery is the **impact you have on others**. The deeper you step into your own strength and presence, the more you'll find yourself inspiring those around you. Your growth and evolution ripple outward, influencing others in ways you may not fully comprehend.

You become a model for the men and women who watch you—whether consciously or unconsciously. As you embody high-vibration masculinity, leadership, and authenticity, you create space for others to rise to their own potential. Your journey of mastery becomes a **living legacy**, inspiring future generations to continue the work you've begun.

With every step you take, you are not just mastering your own life but influencing the world around you in profound ways. And this impact extends beyond your immediate circle—it ripples out into the broader community, the workplace, and even society at large. By **living with integrity** and **purpose**, you become part of a **larger movement** that fosters strength, authenticity, and respect in the world.

◆ The Final Thought: Embrace the Journey

Ultimately, the path to mastery is not about perfection—it's about **commitment**. The journey is lifelong, but that's what makes it so rewarding. Each day offers new opportunities to refine, grow, and evolve. There will be setbacks and triumphs, challenges and breakthroughs. But it's the process itself—the dedication to continual improvement—that makes this journey worth taking.

You will never truly "arrive" at mastery. But you will grow into the person you're meant to be by **staying true to the principles of masculine frame** and **living with integrity and authenticity**. This journey, with its twists and turns, will shape you into a man whose **presence is unwavering**, whose influence is profound, and whose legacy will endure long after you've walked this earth.

Embrace the journey. **Become the frame**. And know that the path of mastery, though challenging, is the most rewarding pursuit you can embark upon.

Walking the World Differently

To **walk the world differently** is to step into each moment with a sense of **purpose, power, and awareness** that transforms how you interact with everyone and everything around you. It's not just about the physical act of walking—it's about how your presence **radiates** and how the world responds to your energy. When you embody the masculine frame, you **shift the energy** in the room as soon as you enter. You **move through life** with a grounded sense of confidence that others instinctively recognize and respect.

The man who walks the world differently does not simply **exist in the world**; he **shapes it**. His actions, words, and demeanor have an undeniable impact, because they are aligned with his deepest essence. He is not trying to prove himself, nor is he seeking validation from others. Instead, he is firmly rooted in his own **sense of purpose and integrity**, and this radiates outwards, subtly influencing everything he encounters.

◆ Presence Over Performance

When you walk through life as a man grounded in masculine frame, you begin to realize that **presence is more important than performance**. Many people live their lives in a state of reaction, constantly performing to meet external expectations or seeking approval from others. They are driven by the need to be noticed, to be validated. In contrast, a man who walks the world differently knows that **his value is intrinsic**, and it is from this understanding that his true power arises.

This **calm confidence** is not the result of external accomplishments or recognition. It is the outcome of a man who has worked hard to **forge an unshakable internal foundation**—one built on authenticity, discipline, and high-vibration masculinity. When you are rooted in these principles, you no longer need to "perform" to prove yourself. **Your presence** alone speaks volumes.

In practical terms, this means that you no longer enter rooms filled with anxiety or the need to be noticed. You enter with **unwavering calm**, confident that your very presence is enough to command attention, respect, and admiration. **You let your actions and energy speak for you**, and in doing so, you shift the energy of the space you occupy.

◆ Moving with Purpose

Walking the world differently also means moving with a deeper **sense of purpose**. Every action, every step, becomes an intentional expression of your core values and your masculine frame. You don't move through life idly or passively. Instead, you walk with direction, knowing who you are and where you are going.

Whether it's in your personal relationships, your career, or your community, every decision you make is **purpose-driven**. Your actions are aligned with your vision, and that alignment creates a sense of **momentum** that others can't help but notice. **Purposeful movement** is magnetic—it pulls people toward you because they can sense that you are someone who has a clear vision and a deep commitment to fulfilling it.

This sense of purpose also gives you the **freedom to navigate the world without hesitation**. When you walk with purpose, you are not easily swayed by distractions or external influences. You know what you stand for, and you move confidently in the direction of your goals. This certainty allows you to remain **grounded** in the face of external pressures, and to **remain focused** on what truly matters to you.

◆ A Quiet Authority

As you walk the world differently, you will find that your authority no longer needs to be asserted aggressively. Instead, it is **conveyed quietly**, through the **strength of your presence** and the **clarity of your vision**. People will begin to sense your **quiet power**, even before you speak.

This kind of authority doesn't require loud declarations or dominance. It is built on the **consistency of your actions** and the **depth of your character**. The more you live in alignment with your values, the more your authority will become a **natural extension of who you are**. You won't have to force respect—it will follow you because you **embody it** effortlessly.

People will be drawn to your ability to stay calm under pressure, to make decisions with clarity, and to lead with confidence. This form of leadership doesn't rely on bravado or intimidation—it is built on the silent force of **integrity, wisdom, and groundedness**. You lead not by dictating, but by showing the way through your actions, inspiring others to follow.

◆ The Power of Subtle Influence

Walking the world differently is also about realizing the power of **subtle influence**. You don't have to shout to be heard; you don't have to force people to follow you. Your influence grows from the strength of your inner frame and the clarity of your purpose.

Subtle influence is the ability to guide, inspire, and impact others **without direct confrontation or overt manipulation**. It's about creating a **space** for others to elevate themselves simply by being around you. People will naturally gravitate toward your energy because they recognize that you **embody something deeper**, something they may not fully understand but instinctively admire.

This kind of influence is not about coercion; it's about **leading by example**, and it's the kind of leadership that **has a lasting impact**. By being authentic, grounded, and aligned with your own purpose, you inspire others to find their own path to power and greatness.

◆ A Legacy of Impact

Ultimately, walking the world differently is not just about how you move through the world today—it's about **the impact you leave behind**. As you embody the masculine frame, you become a beacon for others, and your presence begins to **shape the spaces you inhabit**. You create a ripple effect that reaches beyond your immediate circle, inspiring those around you to rise to their own potential.

When you walk with purpose, presence, and authenticity, you don't just change the way you live—you change the way others live too. You create a world in which strength is measured not by force, but by the quiet power of authenticity, groundedness, and integrity. You become a **living testament** to the kind of man the world needs: someone who is confident, resilient, and deeply connected to his truth.

The way you walk through the world becomes your **legacy**. It's not the titles you hold or the accolades you collect—it's the **energy you leave behind**, the way you inspire those around you, and the lives you touch along the way.

Walking the world differently is not just about how you present yourself to others; it's about how you **show up for yourself**. It's about embodying your true power, walking with unwavering purpose, and becoming a force of positive influence wherever you go. When you embrace the masculine frame and walk the world with intention, you not only shape your own destiny but the destiny of everyone you encounter.

Final Words to the Grounded Man

To the man who has embarked on the journey of mastering his masculine frame, these final words are both a reminder and a challenge. The path you have chosen is not an easy one, but it is a path that will bring you **unshakable strength**, **authenticity**, and a deep sense of **purpose**.

A grounded man is not someone who is passive or indifferent to the world around him. On the contrary, he is a man who has learned to **stand firm in his truth**, who moves through the world with **unwavering calm** and an **open heart**. He is aware of his power, but he chooses to wield it with intention, never seeking to dominate or control, but to influence and inspire.

◆ The Power of Quiet Strength

As a grounded man, your strength comes from within. It is not loud or boisterous, nor is it dependent on external validation. It is a deep, internal knowing that **you are enough** as you are. Your strength is the strength of someone who has **faced his fears**, **embraced his flaws**, and learned to stand tall in the face of adversity.

This strength does not need to prove itself to anyone. It **simply is**. It's a strength that allows you to face the challenges of life with resilience, knowing that **you have everything within you** to handle whatever comes your way. You move through the world **with purpose**, and others will take note of the quiet, powerful energy you radiate.

◆ Trust in the Process

Remember that **mastery is a lifelong journey**, not a destination. Each day offers an opportunity to deepen your understanding of yourself, to refine your actions, and to live more fully in alignment with your core values. It is in the **daily practice** of self-discipline, emotional control, and authenticity that you build the foundation of your masculine frame.

There will be times when the road feels long or when doubt creeps in, but trust that every step you take brings you closer to the man you are destined to be. **Your journey is unique**, and while others may walk a different path, the strength of your frame will be built through your **own experiences** and **choices**.

Trust in the process, and in the work you're doing every single day. The man you are becoming will not be defined by how fast you get there, but by the **depth of your journey**.

◆ Lead with Integrity

As you continue on this journey, lead with **integrity**. Integrity is the cornerstone of your masculinity. It is the quality that will allow you to walk through life with **authenticity** and **respect**—both for yourself and others. When you are rooted in integrity, you are not swayed by the whims of others, the approval of the masses, or the fleeting distractions of modern life. You are led by your own **inner compass**.

This integrity will set you apart. It will be the foundation upon which your **influence** and **respect** are built. The men and women around you will gravitate toward you because they will sense the strength in your character, the steadiness in your actions, and the unwavering commitment you have to your own truth.

◆ The Legacy You Leave Behind

As you continue to evolve, always remember that **the true measure of your life will not be in what you accumulate,** but in the legacy you leave behind. The **mark you leave on the world** will be defined by how you show up every single day, how you lead with authenticity, and how you influence others with your grounded power.

A grounded man's legacy is not defined by the amount of money he makes, the titles he holds, or the recognition he receives. His legacy is built through the relationships he nurtures, the integrity he embodies, and the way he makes others feel when they are in his presence. You are **building that legacy now**, through every decision you make and every action you take.

◆ The Grounded Man in the World

The world is hungry for grounded men—men who have done the work to know themselves, men who lead with purpose and integrity, men who influence not through force, but through their presence and authenticity. When you become that man, you not only **change your life**, but you change the lives of those around you. You become a beacon for others, guiding them toward their own sense of strength, purpose, and truth.

Remember, being grounded doesn't mean being passive. It means being **fully present**, standing tall in your own truth, and moving with intentionality. It means facing each day with courage, knowing that you have everything within you to overcome any challenge that comes your way. It means embracing your **power** while maintaining a sense of **humility**, and using your influence to **uplift others** rather than seeking to control them.

◆ The Final Thought

As you step forward into the world, know this: **you are enough**. You are worthy of respect, worthy of love, and worthy of all the abundance that life has to offer. The journey of becoming the grounded man you are meant to be is one that will never truly end. It is a lifelong pursuit of growth, evolution, and **living with purpose**.

So, walk with your head held high. Walk with a **steel spine** and a **calm heart**. Walk as the man who knows his worth, who understands the power of his presence, and who leads with quiet confidence and strength. Your journey has only just begun.

www.ingramcontent.com/pod-product-compliance
Lightning Source LLC
Chambersburg PA
CBHW021232130626
46554CB00004B/1455